THE GERMAN PASTRY BAKEBOOK

THE GERMAN PASTRY BAKEBOOK

Margit Stoll Dutton

Chilton Book Company
Radnor, Pennsylvania

Copyright © 1977 by Margit Stoll Dutton
All Rights Reserved
Published in Radnor, Pennsylvania, by Chilton Book Company
and simultaneously in Don Mills, Ontario, Canada,
by Thomas Nelson & Sons, Ltd.
Designed by Warren Infield
Photography by Christian Teubner, Füssen, West Germany
Manufactured in the United States of America

Library of Congress Cataloging in Publication Data

Dutton, Margit Stoll.
   The German pastry bakebook.

   Includes index.
   1. Pastry 2. Cookery, German. I. Title.
TX773.D83 1977   641.8'65   77-6148
ISBN 0-8019-6564-0

For my family—on both sides of the Atlantic

Contents

Preface   ix

Utensils and Ingredients   1
    Pans for Baking   1
    About the Oven   2
    Flour   2
    Eggs   3
    Egg Whites   4
    Butter   5
    Cream   5
    Sugar   6
    Salt   7
    Nuts   7
    Vanilla   8
    Fruit   9
    Chocolate   10
    Some Remarks on Nutrition   10

Rührkuchen (butter and pound cakes)   11
    Pans for *Rührkuchen*   11
    Preparing the Batter   11
    Baking the Cake   13
    Unmolding Cakes   14
    Serving the Cake   14
    When Things Go Wrong   14
    Recipes   15-30

Obstkuchen und flache Kuchen (tarts)   31
    Mürbteig (rich tart pastry)   31
    Directions for Making *Mürbteig*   34
        Rolling and Shaping the Dough   35
        Lining the Pan   36
        Baking the Tart Shell   36
        Unmolding Tarts   37
        When Things Go Wrong   37
    Recipes   *38-61*

Biskuit (spongecake)   63
    Preparing the Pan   63
    Preparing the Batter   64
        Making Butter Spongecake   66
    In the Oven   66
    Unmolding a *Biskuit*   66
    Some Serving Ideas   67
    Recipes   *68-74*

Torten (tortes)   75
    Filling a Torte   75
    Frosting a Torte   76
    About Decorating   76
    About Storage and Freezing   77
    Slicing a Torte   77
    Recipes   *78-99*

Brandteig (cream puff pastry)   101
    Cream Puff Pastry Dough   101
    Recipes   *102-103*

Strudel   105
    Strudel Dough   105
    Recipes   *107-109*

Blätterteig (puff pastry)   111
    Puff Pastry Dough   111
    Puff Pastry Shell for Tarts   114
    Recipes   *115-120*

Hefeteig (yeast dough)   121
    Preparing the Dough   121
    Making Yeast Dough   122
    Yeast Dough Shell for Tarts   124
    Yeast Dough Base for Sheet Tarts and Cakes   124
    Recipes   *125-139*

Kleingebäck (cookies)   *141*
    About Baking and Storing   *141*
    Recipes   *141-147*

Toppings, Frostings, Fillings, and Decorative Candies   *149*
    Streusel   *149*
    Quark   *149*
    Buttercreams   *151*
    Schlagsahne (whipped cream)   *157*
    Custard Fillings for Tarts   *160*
    Fondant and Sugar Frostings   *161*
    Glazes   *166*
    Candies, *Krokant,* Nougat, Marzipan, Candied Orange
      and Lemon Peel   *167-174*

Glossary   *175*

Sources of Baking Equipment and Supplies   *176*

Index   *177*

Preface

Does a love for fine baking run in a family? For years, I wouldn't have thought so myself. Even after I had left school in Germany and was out on my own, there was no incentive for me to care particularly about baking, since trips back home—or just to the local *Konditorei*—were enough to satisfy my love for good pastries. It was not until after I moved to the United States that I began to miss the marvels of German pastry. I wanted to try my hand at them for the pleasure of my family and friends. So started my career as a German "home baker."

Baking has become much easier over the years with mixers that beat a cake perfectly in a short time, ovens that can be exactly set, and freezers which enable us to do much preparation in advance. Not that some of the old ways were without their charm: I can still remember as a child seeing homemade dough being loaded on a little wooden cart and wheeled to the local *Bäckerei* to be baked. My mother insisted that breads and sweet yeast pastries finished in the baker's huge brick oven always tasted better than those done at home!

The story shows how seriously the Germans tend to take the making of their baked goods. Whether the context is an afternoon *Kaffeeklatsch* at the home of a friend, or a leisurely hour spent in a *Konditorei-Cafe,* one is inevitably struck by the time and care—not to mention fine ingredients—the Germans lavish on their astonishingly varied cakes and pastries.

Many of the recipes in this book have been handed down from my mother and grandmother. These, as well as other traditional recipes, have been carefully adapted and tested for American kitchens. To ensure best possible results, read the introductory material at the start of each section and scan each recipe before you begin. Follow the recipes closely, and you will be certain to succeed. Still, there is a German saying to be borne in mind: *Kein Meister ist vom Himmel gefallen*—experts don't fall out of the sky. There is much to be learned about German baking as you go along, but the results, you will find, more than justify the effort.

Guten Appetit!

Utensils and Ingredients

Pans for Baking

Springform Pans

The single pan most used in this book is the springform pan. Delicate tortes, cakes, and tarts are sometimes difficult to remove from the pan without breaking. The springform pan solves this problem with its removable rim which fits snugly into the grooves of its bottom.

Most springform pans are imported from West Germany. The best quality pans are of tinned steel. If you are buying a springform set, it will have three interchangeable bottoms: a flat bottom (either smooth or waffle-textured), a flat bottom with a central tube, and a fluted bottom with a tube. Most of the time the flat bottom is the one to use, though the others are handy.

Recipes call variously for springform pans of 8-inch, 9-inch, and 10-inch sizes. Each pan is about 2½ inches deep.

Gugelhopf or Turk's Head Mold

The traditional mold for making *Gugelhopf* is a fluted pan with a central tube. The tube conducts heat so that heavier doughs and batters will cook well in the center.

These molds are made and imported from West Germany. A heavy-gauge tinned steel pan is the best to buy.

Recipes in this book are designed for a 9 to 10-inch diameter *Gugelhopf* mold.

Rehrücken (saddle of venison) Mold

This pan is used for the rich chocolate nut log on page 93. It is ribbed and measures 12 inches long and 4¾ inches wide. You may use this mold for other cakes, as well as for bread.

Loaf Pans

The following loaf pans are used throughout the book for pound cakes and some yeast bakery. Sizes 9 x 5 x 3 inches, 10 x 5 x 3 inches, 13 x 5 x 3½ inches, and 14 x 4½ x 2¾ inches.

Jelly Roll Pan

If you make spongecake rolls often, you will want this pan especially designed for the job. The one-inch sides keep the batter from running off as it would with an ordinary baking sheet. If no jelly roll pan is available, construct your own, using heavy aluminum foil which is then set on a baking sheet.
Size: 16 x 11 x 1 inch high.

Baking Sheets

You will need one or more of these. Any size is suitable for small pastries; a 16 x 14-inch baking sheet is perfect for Strudel and other recipes.

About the Oven

Whether your oven is gas or electric, old or new, expensive or inexpensive—all of this is unimportant compared with knowing your oven's heat distribution and exact temperature. Since so many ovens have inaccurate settings, I strongly recommend the use of an oven thermometer. When baking a delicate pastry, a setting error as small as 25°F can make a difference, so it is best to know your oven's temperature exactly.

All the recipes in this book have been tested in my own ancient gas oven. It has four racks, and for most pastries my own best luck has been with the lowest rack. If your racks are spaced differently than mine, or if you have an electric oven, you may get better results by moving up to the lower-middle area of the oven. It is impossible to be very specific about this problem; try out alternatives to decide the best course for your situation. But whatever you do, preheat the oven for 10 to 15 minutes, and always place the pan in the center of the rack.

Mehl (flour)

Three different types of flour are used in this book: all-purpose bleached, all-purpose unbleached, and cake flour.

It is important to measure flour as accurately as possible. I have found a set of nested aluminum or stainless steel measuring cups is best for the task. The following system is used throughout this book:

1. In recipes calling for "sifted flour," place the correct size cup on a piece of wax paper or foil and sift the flour into it until it overflows. With

the back of a straight knife, sweep off the excess flour, leveling it. Do not tap or shake the cup.

2. In recipes simply stating "flour," merely fill the correct size cup with flour until it overflows, sweeping off the excess to level it.

Sifted and unsifted flour give different measurements. While flour for yeast dough or rich tart pastry does not need sifting, other more sensitive batters requiring aeration must have sifted flour.

All-purpose Bleached Flour. This flour is a blend of hard and soft wheats. Hard wheat is high in protein, which forms the gluten to give the elastic quality desirable in yeast doughs or simple cakes. Its high gluten factor makes it unsuitable for very light and delicate cakes.

All-purpose Unbleached Flour. Unbleached flour is even higher in gluten, and I prefer this flour for making yeast doughs, rich tart pastry, or strudel dough. It looks somewhat yellowish in color, chiefly because of carotenoid pigments, and it has not been chemically treated. If you cannot find this flour, you may substitute the bleached variety.

Cake Flour. Prepared from soft wheat, this flour has a high starch content and is low in gluten. It is finely milled, feels soft and satiny to the touch, and is an ideal flour for delicate, fine-textured cakes and tortes. If only all-purpose flour is available, substitute cornstarch for one-third of the flour in all the recipes calling for cake flour.

Cornstarch. Sometimes cornstarch is mixed with flour to weaken the gluten content, or used in custards where it acts as a thickener.

Farina. This high-protein cereal made from hard wheat is occasionally called for in German baking. If possible, do not use the "instant" kind.

Eier (eggs)

For cakes or any other food, eggs give flavor, color, structure, and texture, besides naturally contributing to food value. They have an important function in baking as a leavening agent, often acting as the only source of leavening.

In this book, recipes calling for eggs are designed for those graded "large," weighing about 2 ounces. Good quality, fresh eggs are necessary for success in baking. The yolk of a fresh egg stands high and the white clings to it in a well-formed mass. A stale egg has a watery white and the yolk is flat. Eggs can best be beaten to their proper volume when they are at room temperature (around 75°F). Egg yolks do not freeze well, but whites can be frozen and used as fresh egg whites.

How to separate an egg: You need three bowls—one for the whites, one for the yolks, and a third small bowl over which the eggs can be broken. Crack the egg and part the shell gently while holding it over the small bowl. Most of the white will immediately fall into the bowl, but continue carefully to pour the yolk back and forth between the two halves of shell, letting additional white glide into the bowl. Place the yolk into the bowl reserved for yolks, and the white into the one set aside for whites. By using the third small bowl you ensure that if a yolk accidentally breaks into the white it will ruin only one egg, and not all the previously accumulated whites. (Egg whites cannot be properly beaten if the slightest amount of yolk is present.)

Egg Whites

In spite of the culinary mystique surrounding methods for achieving perfectly beaten egg whites, the operation is easy once its principles are understood. While yeast, baking powder, and other leavening agents make a cake rise by the release of carbon dioxide as the cake bakes, egg whites perform the task in a simpler way. Beaten egg whites are more air than egg, consisting of countless tiny bubbles. When heat is applied to these, they expand, causing the cake to rise. The success of your cake thus depends on how much air you are able to beat into the whites, and how well you are able to fold them into the batter without deflating them.

Perfectly beaten egg whites have a smooth texture and velvety sheen and, when done, should stand in stiff peaks. If the whites are to be beaten by hand, a wire whip should be used, but any sort of electric beater will work very well. The bowl should be round-bottomed and is best if made of stainless steel. Plastic is adequate if it is very carefully washed beforehand—otherwise, trace amounts of oil or fat clinging to it will interfere with the rising of the whites. Porcelain and glass bowls should be avoided: their slippery surfaces do not support the rising whites.

If egg whites have a reputation for being finicky about deciding whether or not they want to rise, it is probably because they are so sensitive to impurities, such as grease or oil, on the bowl or beater. The tiniest amount of yolk in the whites will also keep them from mounting properly. Chilled egg whites should be allowed to stand at room temperature for at least 20 minutes before beating, otherwise they will not mount sufficiently.

Beating the Egg Whites

By Hand. Start beating with a wire whip at a rate of about two strokes per second in a vertical circular motion. When the whites have begun to foam, add ¼ teaspoon cream of tartar for every six eggs. Continue the beating, rotating the bowl occasionally so that all of the liquid whites are beaten into the fluff. When you think the whites are sufficiently beaten, hold up the whip with a dollop of whites on the end. If the peak stays firm, you have achieved "stiffly beaten egg whites." If not, continue a bit longer and test again. Beaten egg whites should be immediately folded into the batter.

By Mixer. Start beating on low until whites begin to foam. Add ¼ teaspoon cream of tartar. Gradually increase speed, and test for stiffness as explained above.

Folding in the Egg Whites

Never use a mixer for folding in egg whites. A wire whip or spatula is best for this task. Fold about one-third of the egg whites into the batter first, then follow with the rest. Cut through the batter and egg whites, going down to the bottom of the bowl and coming up along the side, thus turning over a portion of the batter. Repeat this motion until whites are folded in. Work quickly, so as not to deflate the egg white bubbles.

Butter

German butter is made from matured cream and tends to have a stronger, nuttier flavor than American butter. Butter is never salted in Germany, and so I have stressed the use of unsalted butter throughout this book. If lightly salted butter is the only kind available, you may substitute it and not add any additional salt to the recipe. This will, however, change the authentic taste of the pastry somewhat.

Fresh, good-quality butter should not be replaced with other shortenings because of the distinctive flavor and texture it imparts to pastries and baked goods. If, however, for health reasons it is necessary to substitute, use unsalted margarine.

Süsse Sahne (whipping or heavy cream)

These days, when "shelf life" means so much to the giant food chains, it is getting harder and harder to find decent whipping cream. In my area there is only one chain store left that carries whipping cream without added "mono and diglycerides, guar gum, carrageenan, and cellulose gum." Besides throwing in these additives to make thin cream more viscous, the milk producers have taken to what they call "ultra pasteurization." This results in a cream which not only does not whip well but which features a distinctly soapy taste.

If you have a choice between "embalmed" heavy cream and the untreated kind, do not hesitate to choose the latter. Good whipping cream can have a fat content of anywhere between 30 percent and 40 percent and should be kept refrigerated. When it is whipped, it must be thoroughly chilled, as should the bowl and beater you use, since a low temperature helps the cream to gain volume. On a very hot day, you may whip cream over ice.

If you are unable to find decent whipping cream commercially, try the following recipe, which I owe to Mrs. Jitka Mencik. She used it in her native Czechoslovakia when she was unable to obtain cream. All it requires is sweet butter, milk, and a blender. For 1¼ cups whipping (or heavy) cream, making 2½ cups whipped:

¾ cup whole milk
½ cup (1 stick) unsalted butter

Place milk and butter into a saucepan. Over low heat, let the butter melt into the milk.
Pour this mixture into a blender jar and blend at the highest speed for 2 minutes.
Refrigerate for 24 hours. Whip cream as you would any commercial whipping cream.

If you plan to use the whipped cream to make decorations with a pastry bag, you may wish it a big stiffer. See then the recipe Whipped Cream with Gelatin.

Sour Cream

Once you have good whipping cream on hand, you will be surprised how utterly delicious home-made sour cream can be. Unlike the commercial type, this sour cream will whip up like whipping cream. (Chill before whipping.) For about 1⅓ cups sour cream, making 2¼ cups when whipped:

1¼ cups whipping cream
3 tablespoons buttermilk (without such additives as tapioca, etc., or it will not thicken properly)

Add the buttermilk to the whipping cream and stir to blend. (Cream does not need refrigeration after the mixing of the butter and milk.)
Let stand at room temperature for at least 24 hours. It will be thick and smell slightly sour.

It may be used right away or be refrigerated for several weeks. The sour cream will become better with age.

Zucker (sugar)

Pliny called sugar "a kind of honey made with reeds," thus describing it in terms of the sweetener he and his fellow Romans knew best. In northern Europe, honey was the only known sweetener until the Crusaders brought back sugar from Syria and Palestine. As trade to the Orient increased in the thirteenth century, this precious substance was greatly sought after for the tables of kings and barons.

In baking, sugar is important far beyond its ability to sweeten. By interfering with the production of gluten, it tends to tenderize cakes and make them rise somewhat higher. In yeast goods, it provides food for yeast. It helps give many cakes a beautiful brown color by caramelizing. Sugar also contributes to the fine texture of cakes, especially those using many eggs.

Cane and beet sugars are both sucrose, and for baking I have noticed no superiority of the former, despite its higher price. It is important, however, that sugar dissolve easily when creamed with butter and that it melt during baking, so one must use fine or very fine granulated sugar. Lumps formed during storage can usually be broken apart. If that does not work, try sifting them or forcing them through a colander.

Confectioners (or powdered) sugar has starch added to it to prevent the formation of lumps. Aside from its uses in frostings, it is excellent simply dusted (through a sieve) over a cake before it is served.

Salz (salt)

Salt plays a very minor role in German pastry making. Here and there a pinch, but nothing beyond that.

Nüsse (nuts)

Nuts are the essential luxury of German baking. They are used whole, sliced, slivered, chopped, or ground, for everything from batters to frostings. In some tortes they are even a complete substitute for flour. Nuts provide flavor and texture and make wonderful decorations. German baking most commonly calls for filberts, almonds, and walnuts.

Always buy fresh, unsalted nuts. Store them in a cool, dry place or, particularly if they have been ground, keep them in a closed container in the refrigerator or freezer. When frozen, they keep many months without becoming rancid.

Grinding Nuts. For medium or fine grinding, use a nut grinder or a Mouli Grater with interchangeable drums. The hand-held Mouli Grater is imported from France and is available in many department stores or specialty shops that carry kitchen equipment. If you do a lot of grinding, a nut grinder you can fasten to a counter top is handier and easier to operate. There are some electric grinders available, in addition to grating attachments for use with electric mixers. These are by far the easiest to use.

It is important that none of the oil be pressed out of the nuts as they are ground. This is why meat grinders and, except for making almond paste, electric blenders are unsatisfactory for nut grinding. The ground nuts should be dry, light, and airy, not pasty looking and mashed together.

Depending on whether they are whole, slivered, or ground, a 4-ounce package of nuts will equal slightly more or less than three-fourths of a cup.

Mandeln (almonds)

Almonds are available in a variety of forms; canned or in cellophane, blanched or unblanched, whole, slivered, or sliced, and in specialty stores even ground.

Some of the recipes using almonds call for the addition of almond extract. This is derived from bitter almonds, which are generally unavailable in this country, though they can be had in Germany. If you do use extract, use it sparingly since it is so potent.

Blanched Almonds. To blanch shelled almonds, drop them into boiling water and boil for a minute. Drain and squeeze each almond out of its skin by pressing between thumb and forefinger. Let them dry a day or two before grinding, or if they must be used immediately, place them in a 350°F oven for 5 minutes.

Toasted Almonds. Place almonds on a baking sheet in a 350°F oven until they are an even, light toasty brown. Whole almonds take 10 to 15 minutes, almond slices only 5 to 8 minutes. If you prefer, you may toast them in a skillet over medium heat, but you must be careful not to burn them.

Sliced or Slivered Almonds. These are sometimes combined with fillings or used for decorations. Difficult to produce at home, they are available packaged in most grocery stores.

Haselnüsse (filberts)

Filberts are native to Germany. The European variety is cultivated in this country under the name "filbert," while its wild cousin is called "hazelnut," in German *Haselnüss*. Though unshelled filberts can be had in health markets at Christmas time, I generally purchase shelled filberts in health food stores where they are available all year long.

Unless otherwise indicated, the nut is used with the rough brown skin on. This adds flavor, color, and texture. If you wish to remove the skin, it is easily done.

Blanched and Toasted Filberts. Spread the nuts on a baking sheet and place in a 350°F oven for about 15 minutes. The skin will flake off and the nut will brown slightly. Take out of the oven and rub the nuts in a folded towel to remove as much of the skin as will come off easily. If you would like them toasted a bit more, return to the oven for a few minutes.

Pistachios

This fine tasting and beautifully colored nut is very popular for decorating tortes and cookies in Germany.

You may find that you are only able to buy pistachios salted in the shell. This is perfectly satisfactory, since blanching will remove the salt.

First shell the nuts—tedious work at best—and drop into boiling water for a minute. Peel off what may be left of the thin, brown skin, trying not to damage the nut.

Pistachios may be chopped with a wide-bladed knife or ground with a nut grinder.

Vanille (vanilla)

Throughout this book pure vanilla extract is designated in the recipes. Unlike Germany, where often only the artificial flavor "vanillin" is available, the pure extract of the vanilla bean can be had anywhere in the United States. I find the taste of extract entirely satisfactory, but if you would rather, you may make your own "vanilla sugar" in the style of German cooks.

8 Utensils and Ingredients

Vanilla Sugar. Buy a vanilla bean—they are usually sold in glass tubes. It should be smooth and black, with a frosting of vanilla crystals. You may open the bean and scrape out the grains, using them to flavor custards, whipped cream, or whatever. Place the rest of the bean into a covered container with granulated or confectioners sugar. In a few weeks you will have a deliciously aromatic vanilla sugar.

Frucht (fruit)

Zitronen und Orangen (lemons and oranges)

Grated lemon peel, and occasionally orange peel, are very important elements in German baking. A difficulty with fresh oranges, and sometimes lemons, is that the peels are often artificially colored and not stamped as such. The best you can do is to look carefully before buying: avoid oranges which appear unnaturally bright in color or have a peculiar unpleasant smell (lemons sometimes have this smell too).

Since the Germans use so much grated and candied citrus peel, their markets offer two different kinds of fruit: treated fruit for juicing and eating and untreated (a little more expensive) for use in baking. Try to find naturally colored fruit and, of course, always use real lemon or orange juice if a recipe calls for it.

Äpfel (apples)

For German apple desserts you need a crisp, tart apple whose flavor can survive being baked. Many apples, such as Red or Golden Delicious, are fine eating apples but they do not have a strong apple flavor. The result can be a lackluster pastry. But experiment with what is available in your area.

To prepare apples, peel, core, and quarter medium-sized apples. If the apples are large, cut them into eighths. Score each piece of apple with three long, shallow slits down the curve. This gives your cake or tart the authentic look.

Toss the sliced apples with sugar and lemon juice so they will not discolor. Let them stand up to one hour to give up juice before using.

Rosinen und Korinthen (raisins and currants)

Raisins. When a recipe calls for raisins, use the seedless type.

Sultanas. These raisins are produced from a yellow seedless grape. If you cannot find them under this name, use the so-called Golden Seedless raisins available in most markets.

Currants. The word originally referred to a small seedless grape and its resulting raisin, which was brought into Europe from Greece. In fact, "currant" is a corruption of "Corinth."

To plump raisins and currants, place them in boiling water for one or two minutes. You will see the flesh puffing up. Drain in a colander and dry them in a towel before using.

Schokolade (chocolate)

For most recipes I have tried to approximate the taste of German baking chocolate by specifying semisweet chocolate together with a small amount of unsweetened chocolate. If you prefer, use only the semisweet type. The recipes are not, however, designed for sweet chocolate.

Chocolate is used both melted and grated. When melting chocolate always use a double boiler. Even with this precaution, it is wise to work over a low flame so that the chocolate will not become grainy.

Grating chocolate is very easily done with a nut grater. Hold the grater over a large platter or bowl, because the chocolate tends (perhaps because of static electricity) to fly in all directions.

Cocoa. In recipes that call for cocoa, use the unsweetened Dutch type, which is very dark in color.

Some Remarks on Nutrition

Something about nutrition in a baking book? And why not? Pastry made with substantial ingredients is not mere junk food. As part of a balanced diet, an occasional piece of pastry in the afternoon or as the coda to a fine meal can be as nutritional as it is good to eat.

In planning a meal, think carefully about what kind of pastry to serve. If the meal is to be a rich one, avoid cakes and tortes made with lots of butter or those which depend on a buttercream. Try instead a spongecake torte filled with custard and topped with fresh fruit, or serve a fruit tart. If you or a member of your family is on a diet which restricts the intake of saturated fat, serve a dessert using a nonbutter spongecake or one of the delicious baked goods which use yeast. In any of the recipes calling for butter, you may substitute unsalted margarine which is usually available in the freezer section of your market.

Speaking of nutrition, here are some of the vital components contained in the basic baking ingredients. Besides fat, butter provides vitamins A and E and calcium. Beyond those, eggs contain vitamins D and B_2, pantothenic acid, biotin, thiamin, iron, and, naturally, lots of protein. Nuts are a good source of vitamins and minerals and contain fair amounts of polyunsaturated fats. Milled white flour unfortunately loses most of its vitamins and minerals in the milling process, but the government requires that certain amounts be replaced before it reaches the market. Still, it is advisable to use whole wheat flour for everyday bread consumption.

Rührkuchen

(butter and pound cakes)

Most popular American cakes, in their ingredients and method of preparation, belong to the class known in Germany as *Rührkuchen,* literally, "beaten cake." In old cookbooks these cakes are also called *Napfkuchen* or *Topfkuchen,* meaning that they are made in one bowl. *Rührkuchen* cakes are simple to make, substantial, and satisfying. They travel to the office without crumbling or provide a delightful accompaniment for afternoon coffee.

There are two basic types: *Einfache Rührkuchen* or butter cake, in which baking powder is usually the leavening agent; and *Sandkuchen* or "sand cake," a rich, light *Rührkuchen,* in some versions identical to pound cake. The lightness of this cake depends largely on how much air is beaten into the batter.

Pans

Whatever type of pan you choose for your *Rührkuchen*, pans should be not less than half or more than two-thirds full when they are put into the oven (loaf pans can be a little fuller). Too large a pan will produce a thin, dry cake; if it is too small the center may be doughy or the cake may fall.

Once you have chosen the pan, butter it generously. Sprinkle in flour, then tilt the pan until the entire inside is dusted with a thin flour coating. Reverse the pan over the sink and tap it on the bottom to knock out the excess.

Preparing the Batter

The following pages describe how to make *Einfache Rührkuchen* (butter cake). These basic methods also apply to *Sandkuchen* (sand cake).

Have all ingredients and utensils at room temperature, or about 75°F. Butter should be soft but not melted. If you have forgotten to take the butter out of the refrigerator, cut it into half-inch pieces and place in a mixing bowl over warm water until it softens. Do not let the butter melt.

Cold eggs can be warmed by leaving them in a bowl of warm water for a few minutes.

Sift together the dry ingredients and set aside.

Separate eggs, grind nuts, plump raisins. Once you start mixing you should not have to stop.

Method I: By Hand

You may beat the batter sitting down, with the bowl in your lap. If you prefer to stand, put a moist cloth between the bowl and your working surface to keep it stationary, or use a bowl with a rubber suction ring on the bottom. Beat from the wrist, not the shoulder, for a more even and less tiring stroke.

A wire whip is an absolute necessity, for a wooden spoon won't produce as light a batter. Beat the butter with even strokes until it is smooth and creamy, about the consistency of mayonnaise. Add the sugar gradually, one spoonful at a time, and continue beating until the sugar has dissolved and the mixture does not feel granular when rubbed between your fingers. A grainy batter will not get as fluffy as you want it to be. This part of the beating may take 15 minutes, but remember, the lightness and fine grain of your cake depend on the amount of air incorporated in the batter, so keep going. Add the egg yolks one at a time, beating well after each addition. This step should take another 15 minutes. If you're enjoying the exercise there's no need to stop here. Many a German grandmother will still insist—with the old cookbooks—that cakes should be beaten for no less than an hour!

Fold in the sifted ingredients about one-fourth at a time, continuing to use light strokes. Here it may be easier to use a spatula or a wooden spoon with a hole in the middle. If milk is used, add alternately with the flour mixture, beginning and ending with an addition of flour. Lastly, fold in raisins, nuts, and candied peel. Set aside the batter. In a separate bowl, beat the egg whites until they form stiff peaks (see egg whites, pages 4-5). Fold into the batter very gently.

Method II: Portable (Hand-Held) Electric Mixer

Prepare ingredients and utensils as described. Place the softened butter in a large mixing bowl and cream for about one minute, until it reaches the consistency of mayonnaise. Add the sugar, a spoonful at a time, and continue beating until it is dissolved and the butter-sugar mixture is fluffy. This will take about five minutes.

Unlike Method I, you can use whole instead of separated eggs. The fast, even action of the mixer incorporates enough air to make the batter sufficiently light. However, for especially sensitive batters, such as those with no baking powder, it would be advisable to beat the egg whites separately and fold them in last to ensure lightness.

Add whole eggs or yolks one at a time, allowing about 5 minutes for this step. Throughout the creaming process, occasionally scrape down the batter on the sides of the bowl. At most, the creaming of the butter, sugar, and eggs should take about 12 minutes. When fully creamed, the batter will be light yellow and fluffy.

Fold in the flour by hand with a spatula or a wooden spoon with a hole in the middle, because the mixer may not work efficiently as the batter becomes heavier. Mix in raisins, nuts, or candied peel. Finally, fold in egg whites, if called for, very gently by hand.

Method III: Heavy-Duty Mixer

Prepare ingredients and utensils as described. Place softened butter in the bowl and cream with the wire loop whip attachment 1 to 2 minutes on low speed. Increase speed to medium and add the sugar a spoonful at a time, waiting until each spoonful is completely mixed before adding the next. After all the sugar has been added, run the mixer about 3 minutes longer until the granules are dissolved and the batter is fluffy.

At this point add whole eggs (or egg yolks in specially indicated recipes) one at a time, allowing each to be thoroughly incorporated before adding the next. This will take about 3 minutes. Stop occasionally to scrape down the sides of the bowl. When fully creamed, the batter will be light yellow and fluffy.

Turn off the mixer and change the wire loop whip to the flat beater attachment. Fold in about one-fourth of the dry ingredients. Mix at the lowest speed. If your recipe calls for milk, add it alternately with the rest of the flour, ending with an addition of flour. Keep the mixer on low. Do not beat beyond the point at which the ingredients are thoroughly mixed.

Fold in raisins, nuts, or candied peel. Finally, fold in egg whites, if called for, very gently by hand.

Baking the Cake

Pour the batter immediately into the prepared pan or mold. To distribute the batter evenly, push it gently to the corners and sides with a spatula until it is level, but never pat it down or try to even it by knocking or shaking the pan: you want the batter to keep its fluffiness.

Slide the pan into the oven, placing it in the middle of the rack for even heat distribution. Since a draft may cause the cake to deflate, do not open the oven for at least 30 minutes.

Unmolding Cakes

The cake is done when a cake tester inserted in the middle comes out clean and the top springs back when pressed gently. The top will be lightly browned and the edges will have shrunk slightly from the sides of the pan. If you have no small children, leave the cake in the turned-off oven with the door open for 10 minutes. Otherwise, set the pan in a draft-free place for the same length of time. Then turn the cake out onto a cake rack.

For a springform pan, run a knife around the sides, slowly unbuckle the removable rim, and set aside. Let the cake rest a few minutes to allow moisture to escape. With the point of a knife loosen the bottom of the cake from the bottom of the pan. Then, holding the cake at a slight angle above the wire rack, slide it off the pan bottom and onto the rack.

To unmold from all other cake pans, place the wire rack across the top of the cake pan, resting it on the rim. With one hand firmly on the rack and the other holding the pan (don't forget a potholder!) turn upside down. Now the rack is on the bottom and the cake pan is reversed upon the rack. Give a sharp jerk to the rack and pan to loosen the cake. The cake should slip out onto the rack. *Gugelhopf, Bundt*, and other ring cakes are left reversed.

Serving the Cake

Americans dearly love cake warm from the oven, but a German *Kuchen* is meant to be served after cooling and will need to "set." Only when the flavors have had time to blend and ripen do you get the expected taste. If possible, make the cake a day before you plan to serve it.

Most of these cakes keep for days if well wrapped. Some will keep much longer. The *Rührkuchen* family freezes very well. *Rührkuchen* is often served with a nice spoonful of *Schlagsahne* (whipped cream).

When Things Go Wrong

Curdling. You are making a cake and doing everything right. The butter and sugar mixture is fluffy and the first egg is beaten in. Then, as you put in the next egg, the batter starts to separate and deflate, looking slightly curdled. What to do? Set the mixing bowl in hot water and stir gently and continuously. Soon the curdled look will disappear. Then take the bowl from the hot water and beat the batter about 2 minutes until it regains airiness. Now you can proceed where you left off.

Burning on Top. Especially in cakes containing *Quark* (cheese), the top of the cake may be thoroughly browned before the center is done. Cover the top loosely with a sheet of aluminum foil and allow it to finish baking.

Unmolding the Cake. If the cake sticks to the bottom of the pan, reverse the pan on a cake rack and put a cold, wet cloth over the bottom for a few minutes. This should loosen the cake—if not, repeat the procedure.

Zitronenkuchen (lemon cake)

The fresh lemon taste of this cake, which can be enhanced by a lemon frosting, goes especially well with tea.

Preheat oven to 375°F.
9-inch ring mold — Butter and flour the pan.

BATTER

1 cup (2 sticks) unsalted butter 1¼ cups sugar 5 egg yolks	Cream butter, sugar, and egg yolks, using one of the methods on pages 11-13.
grated peel of 2 lemons juice of 1 lemon strained	Add lemon peel and lemon juice, a spoonful at a time.
2¼ cups sifted flour ¼ cup sifted cornstarch 2 teaspoons baking powder pinch of salt	Mix in flour, cornstarch, baking powder, and salt.
5 egg whites	Beat egg whites separately and fold in delicately.

Pour immediately into the prepared pan and bake on the lowest rack of a preheated 375°F oven for 50 minutes, or until a cake tester inserted in the middle comes out clean. Cool in the pan 10 minutes before turning out onto a cake rack to cool thoroughly.

Serving Suggestions. Dust with confectioners sugar or glaze with a lemon icing of your choice.

Tiroler Kuchen (Tyrolean cake)

Generally speaking, German cooking does not feature complex flavor combinations. An exception is this intriguing cake with its blend of lemon, almonds or filberts, cinnamon, and chocolate.

Preheat oven to 375°F.
9-inch Bundt pan or ring mold — Butter and flour the pan.

BATTER

1 cup (2 sticks) unsalted butter	Cream butter, sugar, and egg yolks, using one of the methods on pages 11-13.
1¼ cups sugar	
6 egg yolks	
grated peel of 1 lemon	Add lemon peel and cinnamon.
1 teaspoon cinnamon	
1¼ cups sifted flour	Mix in sifted flour, baking powder, and salt.
1 teaspoon baking powder	
pinch of salt	
7 ounces (2⅓ cups) semisweet chocolate, medium ground	Add chocolate and nuts.
1½ cups finely ground almonds or filberts	
6 egg whites	Beat egg whites separately and fold in delicately.

Pour immediately into the prepared pan and bake on the lowest rack of a preheated 375°F oven for 60 to 70 minutes, or until a cake tester inserted in the middle comes out clean. Cool in the pan 10 minutes before turning out onto a cake rack to cool thoroughly.

Dust with confectioners sugar.

Marmorkuchen (marble cake)

A substantial cake with a combination of vanilla and rum-flavored chocolate.

Preheat oven to 375°F.
9-inch *Gugelhopf* mold	Butter and flour the pan.

BATTER

1 cup plus 2 tablespoons unsalted butter	Cream butter, sugar, and eggs, using one of the methods on pages 11-13.
1¾ cups sugar	
4 eggs	
1½ teaspoons vanilla extract	Add vanilla.
3⅔ cups sifted flour	Fold in half of the flour and baking powder. Add the milk. Mix in the remainder of flour, stirring gently but thoroughly.
2 teaspoons baking powder	
⅓ cup whole milk	

CHOCOLATE BATTER

3 tablespoons cocoa	Stir cocoa and rum together in a bowl until smooth. Remove one-third of the batter and fold gently into the cocoa mixture.
3 tablespoons dark rum	

Pour half of the remaining vanilla batter into the prepared pan, smoothing it with a spatula. Then add the chocolate portion, followed by the rest of the vanilla batter. If you wish, run a knife blade through the batter to marble it further.

Bake on the lowest rack of a preheated 375°F oven for 55 to 60 minutes, or until a cake tester inserted in the center comes out clean. Cool in the pan for 10 minutes before unmolding onto a cake rack to cool thoroughly.

Dust with confectioners sugar.

Haselnusskuchen (filbert cake)

The feathery quality of ground nuts gives a new texture to the butter cake: lighter, spongier, but not coarser. A chocolate glaze is the perfect complement to the nutty flavor.

Preheat oven to 375°F.
8-inch ring mold   Butter and flour the pan.

BATTER

½ cup plus 2 tablespoons unsalted butter	Cream butter, sugar, and eggs, using one of the methods on pages 11-13.
1¼ cups sugar	
3 eggs	
1 teaspoon vanilla extract	Add vanilla, lemon peel, and salt.
grated peel of ½ lemon	
pinch of salt	
2 cups finely ground filberts	Fold in filberts, flour, and baking powder.
1¼ cups sifted flour	
2 teaspoons baking powder	

Pour immediately into the prepared pan and bake on the lowest rack of a preheated 375°F oven for 45 minutes, or until a cake tester inserted in the center comes out clean. Let the cake cool in the pan for 10 minutes before unmolding onto a wire rack to cool thoroughly.

Serving Suggestions. Dust with confectioners sugar or glaze with chocolate frosting of your choice.

Quark-Napfkuchen (one-bowl cheese cake)

When people first taste this *Kuchen*, they are often unable to account for the flavor. It is *Quark* which provides the unusually tangy taste and velvety texture.

Preheat oven to 375°F.
9-inch springform pan   Butter and flour the pan.

BATTER

1 cup raisins	Plump raisins in boiling water for one or two minutes. Drain, dry, and set aside.
½ cup plus 2 tablespoons unsalted butter 1 cup sugar 3 eggs.	Cream butter, sugar, and eggs, using one of the methods on pages 11-13.
1 teaspoon vanilla extract grated peel of 1 lemon	Add vanilla and lemon peel.
1 cup *Quark* (see page 149.)	Slowly add the *Quark*, one spoonful at a time.
2½ cups sifted flour 3 teaspoons baking powder	Fold in flour and baking powder.
½ cup blanched almonds, medium ground (optional) raisins as above	Dust raisins lightly with flour and fold in last, together with the nuts.

Pour immediately into the prepared pan and bake on the lowest rack of a preheated 375°F oven for 50 minutes, or until a cake tester inserted in the middle comes out clean. Check after 30 minutes, for this cake may brown prematurely. If needed, place a piece of aluminum foil lightly on top of the cake to prevent burning. Cool in the pan 10 minutes before turning out onto a cake rack to cool thoroughly.

Serving Suggestion. Dust generously with confectioners sugar.

Streuselkuchen (crumb cake)

This crumb topping is lightly flavored with cinnamon or grated lemon peel and is full of crispy lumps. For contrast, the cake base in kept simple, with less butter and fewer eggs than in many recipes. If you prefer an even simpler base, substitute the yeast dough on page 124. In Germany both types of *Streuselkuchen* are served.

Preheat oven to 375°F. 9-inch springform pan. For streusel, see page 149.	Butter and flour the pan. Set aside while preparing the batter.

BATTER

½ cup plus 3 tablespoons unsalted butter 1 cup sugar 2 eggs	Cream butter, sugar, and eggs, using one of the methods on pages 11-13.
1 teaspoon vanilla extract grated peel of ½ lemon pinch of salt	Add flavorings and salt.
2½ cups sifted flour 2 teaspoons baking powder	Fold in flour and baking powder.

18   Rührkuchen

Pour the batter immediately into the prepared pan. Spread the streusel topping evenly over the batter. Place on the lowest rack of a preheated 375°F oven and bake for 50 to 60 minutes, or until a cake tester inserted in the center comes out clean. Leave in the pan for 10 minutes before unmolding it onto a cake rack.

Schokoladenkuchen (chocolate nugget cake)

Semisweet chocolate is cut into pieces the size of small peas and stirred into this fine butter cake.

Preheat oven to 375°F.
9-inch *Gugelhopf* pan   Butter and flour the pan.

BATTER

1 cup (2 sticks) unsalted butter	Cream butter, sugar, and eggs, using one of the methods on pages 11-13.
1¼ cups sugar	
4 eggs	
1 teaspoon vanilla extract	Add vanilla.
2½ cups sifted flour	Mix in flour, cornstarch, baking powder, and salt.
½ cup sifted cornstarch	
2 teaspoons baking powder	
pinch of salt	
4 ounces semisweet chocolate, chopped into pea-sized bits	Fold in chocolate bits.

Pour into the prepared pan and bake on the lowest rack of a preheated 375°F oven for 50 minutes, or until a cake tester inserted in the middle comes out clean. Cool in the pan for 10 minutes before unmolding onto a cake rack to cool thoroughly.

Serving Suggestions. Dust with confectioners sugar or glaze with a chocolate frosting of your choice.

Rum Gugelhopf (rum-raisin cake)

In Germany this cake might be made with arrack, an Arabian liqueur. If you can find it, use it! Otherwise, be sure to use dark Jamaican rum for a full-bodied flavor.

Preheat oven to 400°F.	
9-inch *Gugelhopf* mold	Butter and flour the pan.
1 cup sultanas (or raisins)	Pour rum over sultanas and let soak for at least ½ hour
3 tablespoons dark rum	

BATTER

1 cup plus 2 tablespoons unsalted butter	Cream butter, sugar, and eggs, using one of the methods on pages 11-13.
1½ cups sugar	
5 eggs	
grated peel of ½ lemon	Add lemon peel and salt.
pinch of salt	
3¼ cups sifted flour	Fold in two-thirds of the flour, cornstarch, and baking powder.
¼ cup sifted cornstarch	
2 teaspoons baking powder	
3 tablespoons dark rum	Add the rum. Then mix in the rest of the flour.
soaked sultanas as above	Dust sultanas lightly with flour and fold in last.

Pour immediately into the prepared pan and bake on the lowest rack of a preheated 400°F oven for 55 to 60 minutes, or until a cake tester inserted in the middle comes out clean. Cool in the pan 10 minutes, then remove to a cake rack to cool thoroughly.

Serving Suggestions. Sprinkle with confectioners sugar or frost with a rum icing of your choice.

Schokoladenkuchen mit Rum (chocolate rum cake)

A dollop of whipped cream nicely softens the rich chocolate quality of this cake.

Preheat oven to 375°F.

9-inch ring mold	Butter and flour the pan.

BATTER

1 cup (2 sticks) unsalted butter	Cream butter, sugar, and egg yolks, using one of the methods on pages 11-13.
1¼ cups sugar	
4 egg yolks	
2 ounces (½ cup) semisweet chocolate, finely grated	Add chocolate, cocoa, rum, and salt.
5 tablespoons cocoa	
3 tablespoons dark rum	
pinch of salt	
2⅓ cups sifted flour	Mix in flour and baking powder.
2 teaspoons baking powder	
4 egg whites	Beat egg whites separately and fold in delicately.

Pour immediately into the prepared pan and bake on the lowest rack of a preheated 375°F oven for 50 minutes, or until a cake tester inserted in the middle comes out clean. Let it cool in the pan for 10 minutes, then unmold onto a cake rack to cool completely.

Dust with confectioners sugar.

Orangenkuchen (orange cake)

This *Kuchen* has the looks, taste, and ingredients of a torte. Its different orange flavors, for the inside and outside, blend very well together.

Preheat oven to 375°F.
14 x 4½-inch loaf pan   Butter and flour the pan.

BATTER

1 cup plus 3 tablespoons unsalted butter	Cream butter, sugar and eggs, using one of the methods on pages 11-13.
1¼ cups sugar	Note: If, because of the amount of eggs, the mixture starts to separate, add a few tablespoons of cornstarch from the amount measured.
4 egg yolks	
3 eggs	
pinch of salt	
3 tablespoons Cointreau (or other good orange liqueur)	Add peels, juices, liqueur, and salt, adding a tablespoon or so more flour if the mixture separates.
1 tablespoon frozen, concentrated orange juice, thawed	
grated peel of 2 oranges	
grated peel of 1 lemon	
1 tablespoon lemon juice	
1½ cups sifted flour	Mix in remainder of flour and cornstarch. Add almonds and, last of all, the orange peel.
½ cup sifted cornstarch	
1 cup finely ground, blanched almonds	
4 ounces (½ cup) very finely sliced candied orange peel, page 173.	

Pour immediately into the prepared pan and bake on the lowest rack of a preheated 375°F oven for 70 minutes or until a cake tester inserted in the middle comes out clean. Cool in the pan for 10 minutes before unmolding it onto a cake rack to cool thoroughly.

¾ cup sweet orange marmalade	In a saucepan, heat up the marmalade to spreading consistency. Cover top and sides of cake.
½ cup sliced almonds, lightly toasted.	Sprinkle the almonds on the cake while marmalade is still warm.

Tausendjahrkuchen (thousand year cake)

The origin of the name is lost in the mists and aromas of culinary history. The flavor in this unaltered nineteenth-century recipe is delightfully citrus. *Tausendjahrkuchen* can be depended upon to stay moist for a long time.

Preheat oven to 375°F.
10 x 5 x 3-inch loaf pan   Butter and flour the pan.

BATTER

½ cup raisins
¾ cup sultanas
1 cup (2 sticks) unsalted butter
1 cup sugar
5 egg yolks
1 teaspoon vanilla extract
grated peel of 1 lemon
pinch of salt
2½ cups sifted flour
¼ cup diced candied lemon peel, pages 173-174
¼ cup diced candied orange peel, pages 173-174
raisins and sultanas as above
5 egg whites

Plump raisins and sultanas in boiling water for 1 or 2 minutes. Drain, dry, and set aside.
Cream butter, sugar, and egg yolks, using one of the methods on pages 11-13.

Add lemon peel, vanilla, and salt.

Fold in flour.
Dust peels and raisins lightly with flour and add to the mixture.

Beat egg whites separately and fold in gently.

Pour immediately into the prepared pan and bake on the lowest rack of a preheated 375°F oven for about 1 hour and 15 minutes, or until a cake tester inserted in the middle comes out clean. Cool in the pan for 10 minutes before unmolding onto a cake rack to cool thoroughly.

Königskuchen (king cake)

A friend from Louisiana reports that a version of this *Kuchen* is called King Cake in Creole cookery and is traditionally baked in a ring shape for Twelfth Night, or Epiphany. The light, sandy texture makes it quite different from other raisin and citrus flavored cakes.

Preheat oven to 375°F.
10 x 5 x 3-inch loaf pan

Butter and flour the pan.

BATTER

1 cup raisins
1 cup currants
1 cup plus 2 tablespoons (2¼ sticks) unsalted butter
1 cup sugar
4 eggs
1 teaspoon vanilla extract
pinch of salt
2 cups sifted flour
½ cup sifted cornstarch
1 teaspoon baking powder
2 tablespoons dark rum
½ cup diced candied lemon or orange peel, page 173
raisins and currants as above

Plump raisins and currants in boiling water for 1 or 2 minutes. Drain, dry, and set aside.

Cream butter, sugar, and eggs, using one of the methods on pages 11-13

Add vanilla and salt.

Fold in flour, cornstarch, and baking powder alternately with rum.

Dust raisins and currants lightly with flour and fold into mixture together with the candied peel.

22   *Rührkuchen*

Pfirsich-Cremetorte (Peach Cream Torte)

Linzertorte

Pour immediately into prepared pan and bake on the lowest rack of a preheated 375°F oven for about 1 hour and 15 minutes, or until a cake tester inserted in the middle comes out clean. Cool in the pan 10 minutes before turning out onto a cake rack to cool thoroughly.

Dust generously with confectioners sugar.

Margaretenkuchen (daisy cake)

Whether or not you own the flower-shaped cake mold from which this *Kuchen* derives its name, you will enjoy its subtle taste. The distinctive ingredient is marzipan (almond paste), which gives the cake's texture a refreshing roughness.

Preheat oven to 375°F.

9-inch *Gugelhopf* or ring mold	Butter and flour the pan.

BATTER

1 cup plus 4 tablespoons (2½ sticks) unsalted butter	Cream butter, almond paste, sugar, and egg yolks, using one of the methods on pages 11-13.
1 cup marzipan (almond paste), pages 171-173	
⅔ cup sugar	
6 egg yolks	
grated peel of 1 lemon	Add lemon peel and salt.
pinch of salt	
1½ cups sifted flour	Mix in flour and cornstarch.
½ cup sifted cornstarch	
6 egg whites	Beat egg whites separately and fold in delicately.

Pour immediately into the prepared pan and bake on the lowest rack of a preheated 375°F oven for 60 minutes, or until a cake tester inserted in the middle comes out clean. Cool in the pan for 10 minutes, then unmold onto a cake rack to cool thoroughly.

Dust lightly with confectioners sugar.

Walnusskuchen (walnut cake)

Simplicity never tasted so good! Tightly wrapped, this loaf cake keeps well for several days.

Preheat oven to 375°F.

9 x 5 x 3-inch loaf pan	Butter and flour the pan.

BATTER

½ cup plus 5 tablespoons unsalted butter	Cream butter, sugar, and egg yolks, using one of the methods on pages 11-13
1 cup sugar	
3 egg yolks	
1 teaspoon vanilla extract	Add vanilla.
2 cups sifted flour	Mix in flour and salt.
pinch of salt	
1 cup coarsely chopped walnuts	Add walnuts.
3 egg whites	Beat egg whites separately and fold in delicately.

Pour immediately into prepared pan and bake on the lowest rack of a preheated 375°F oven for about 1 hour and 15 minutes, or until a cake tester inserted in the middle comes out clean. Cool in the pan 10 minutes before turning out onto a cake rack to cool thoroughly.

Aniskuchen (anise cake)

Anise is a frequently used spice in German baking; it lends a delicate taste and fragrance to this cake. You may use whole anise seeds instead of ground anise to obtain a seedcake effect.

Preheat oven to 375°F.	
10 x 5 x 3-inch loaf pan	Butter and flour the pan.

BATTER

1 cup (2 sticks) unsalted butter	Cream butter, sugar, and eggs, using one of the methods on pages 11-13.
1 cup sugar	
4 eggs	
1 teaspoon vanilla extract	Add vanilla and salt.
pinch of salt	
3½ cups sifted flour	Mix in half of the flour and baking powder. Add the milk. Fold in the other half of the flour mixture, stirring gently but thoroughly.
3 teaspoons baking powder	
3 tablespoons milk	
1½ tablespoons anise seeds Or	Add anise.
1 teaspoon ground anise	

Pour immediately into the prepared pan and bake on the lowest rack of a preheated 375°F oven for 60 minutes, or until a cake tester inserted in the middle comes out clean. Cool in the pan 10 minutes before turning out onto a cake rack to cool thoroughly.

Rührkuchen

Bienenstich (beehive cake)

This delightful cake, whose name literally means "bee sting," has a golden butter-honey-almond topping. You might also prepare *Bienenstich* baked on a sheet using a yeast dough base, page 124. This cake may be served either filled or unfilled.

Preheat oven to 375°F.
9-inch springform pan   Butter and flour the pan.

TOPPING

4 tablespoons unsalted butter	Melt the butter in a heavy-bottomed saucepan over low heat. Stir in sugar, honey, and cream. Over a low flame, stir the mixture and boil for 5 minutes.
¼ cup sugar	
1½ tablespoons honey	
1 tablespoon whipping cream	
1 cup almonds, blanched and slivered	Add almonds and vanilla. Set the topping aside to cool until it is warm while you make the batter. It will thicken into a heavy syrup.
¼ teaspoon vanilla extract	

BATTER

½ cup plus 3 tablespoons unsalted butter	Cream butter, sugar, and eggs, using one of the methods on pages 11-13.
⅔ cup sugar	
3 eggs	
1 teaspoon vanilla extract	Add vanilla and salt.
pinch of salt	
2½ cups sifted flour	Fold in flour and baking powder.
2 teaspoons baking powder	

Pour the batter immediately into the prepared pan. Spread the topping over the batter, smoothing it with a spatula.

Bake on the lowest rack of a preheated 375°F oven for 35 to 40 minutes, or until a cake tester inserted in the middle comes out clean. Check after 25 minutes, for the topping may brown prematurely. If necessary, place a piece of aluminum foil lightly over the cake. Cool in the pan for 10 minutes, then unmold onto a cake rack to cool completely.

The cake may be served plain or with one of the following fillings:

Buttercream with Custard Base, page 153, flavored with vanilla	Fill a few hours before serving so that the flavors can blend.
Or	
½ pint of whipping cream, flavored with vanilla, page 157	

Assembling the Cake. Splitting the *Bienenstich* requires special care because the top crust is easily broken. Using a long knife, preferably longer than the cake is wide, carefully cut the cake into two layers. Lift an edge of the top layer with the knife and slip a piece of wax paper between the layers. Work the wax paper forward until it is all the way under the top layer. Grasp the overhanging edges of the wax paper on either side, lift off the top layer, and set aside.

Spread the bottom layer with buttercream or whipped cream. Pick up the top layer with the wax paper again and hold it over the filling. Tilt the top until one edge almost touches the edge of the bottom. From here you should be able to slide the wax paper back gradually as you lower the top layer onto the filling.

Versunkener Apfelkuchen (sunken apple cake)

This is a juicy apple topping over a simple butter cake. Try it either way: with an apple or currant glaze or baked with a sprinkling of ground nuts and raisins.

Preheat oven to 375°F.
10-inch springform pan   Butter and flour the pan.

TOPPING

1½ pounds crisp, tart apples, medium sized	Peel, core, and slice apples into eighths. Sprinkle with sugar and lemon juice and stir to coat. Set aside.
1 tablespoon sugar	
2 teaspoons lemon juice	
1 cup finely ground filberts or almonds	Mix nuts and sugar and set aside. Do not mix in raisins.
3 tablespoons sugar	
¼ cup raisins (optional)	

BATTER

1 cup (2 sticks) unsalted butter	Cream butter, sugar, and egg yolks, using one of the methods on pages 11-13.
1 cup sugar	
4 egg yolks	
1 teaspoon vanilla extract	Add vanilla, lemon peel, and salt.
grated peel of ½ lemon	
pinch of salt	
2 cups sifted flour	Mix in flour, cornstarch, and baking powder.
½ cup sifted cornstarch	
2 teaspoons baking powder	
4 egg whites	Beat egg whites separately and fold in gently.

Pour the batter immediately into the prepared pan and smooth with a spatula.

Arrange the apple slices so that they overlap, each on the next, forming concentric circles on top of the cake. Press the slices down slightly, inserting raisins between them. Sprinkle nut-sugar mixture evenly over all.

Place at once in the lower middle of a preheated 375°F oven and bake for 50 minutes, or until a cake tester inserted in the middle comes out clean. Cool in the pan 10 minutes before turning out onto a cake rack to cool thoroughly.

Variations. Omit nut-sugar mixture. Prepare 1½ cups of apple or currant glaze, page 167. Pour the glaze over the cake, let it cool, and serve within the next few hours.

Or sprinkle the cake generously with confectioners sugar after it has cooled.

Serving Suggestion. Serve each piece with a spoonful of *Schlagsahne* (whipped cream).

Versunkener Sauerkirschenkuchen (sunken sour cherry cake)

Every year when the cherries are ripe my sister Gertrud whips up this specialty. She does not remove the cherry pits, which is why this cake is known within our family by the unappetizing name of *Spuckkuchen* (spit cake). But when you taste this cake, its name becomes quite irrelevant.

The cherries should be tart pie cherries (the batter is sweet enough to balance them). For an excellent variation, use tart plums.

Preheat oven to 375°F.	
10-inch springform pan	Butter and flour the pan.
TOPPING	
2½ cups fresh, unpitted cherries Or 1 pound pitted cherries, canned or frozen	Drain cherries well and set aside.
1 teaspoon cinnamon 1 tablespoon sugar	Mix cinnamon and sugar.
BATTER	
1 cup (2 sticks) unsalted butter 1⅓ cups sugar 3 eggs	Cream butter, sugar, and eggs, using one of the methods on pages 11-13.
1 teaspoon vanilla extract Or 1 tablespoon rum	Add vanilla or rum.
2½ cups sifted flour ½ cup sifted cornstarch 2 teaspoons baking powder	Fold in flour, cornstarch, and baking powder.

Pour the batter immediately into the prepared pan and smooth it with a spatula. Distribute the cherries over the batter, pressing each down slightly to anchor it. Sprinkle the cinnamon-sugar mixture evenly over all.

Place at once in the lower middle of a preheated 375°F oven and bake for 50 to 60 minutes, or until a cake tester inserted in the middle comes out clean. Cool in the pan 10 minutes before unmolding it onto a cake rack to cool thoroughly.

Variations. Omit the cinnamon-sugar mixture. Prepare 1½ cups of cherry or plum glaze, page 167. Pour the glaze over the cake and let it cool.

Or sprinkle the cake generously with confectioners sugar after it has cooled.

Serving Suggestion. Serve each piece with a spoonful of *Schlagsahne* (whipped cream).

Sandkuchen (sand cake)

Sandkuchen is an example of what the Germans call a "fine" *Kuchen*, meaning a rich, delicately textured cake made without benefit of baking powder. In some *Sandkuchen* recipes cornstarch is partially substituted for flour; these more crumbly versions are what suggest the cake's name.

Older German cookbooks give what are called *Ei schwer* (literally, "egg weight") recipes for *Sandkuchen*. According to this sensible system, specific amounts of ingredients are not provided; rather everything is given in proportion relative to the weight of the eggs used. It was a helpful technique in the days before grading standards for eggs. The following recipes are converted for the use with ordinary large eggs.

The classical recipe for *Sandkuchen* is a pound cake calling for the same weight each of eggs, flour, butter, and sugar. This recipe is rich indeed, but these proportions can be altered somewhat with the result still being called *Sandkuchen*. With changes of balance it is sometimes necessary to add a small amount of baking powder to insure proper rising. But in any event, since the primary leavening agents are the butter and eggs, it is imperative that they be beaten into a light, fluffy mass. Some recipes call for the addition of rum, and the alcohol will also help lighten the cake.

Traditionally *Sandkuchen* is served with a dusting of confectioners sugar or glazed with a frosting. A frosting will help keep the cake fresh and moist longer, besides adding flavor to it. A chocolate, rum, or lemon frosting is best for this type of cake.

Sandkuchen can be baked in either a loaf, ring, or springform pan. Whatever is used, however, the pan should be lined with aluminum foil or baking parchment prior to baking. This is particularly easy to accomplish if you sculpture the foil around the outside of the inverted pan before trying to shape it to the inside. Butter the foil lightly.

Do not open the oven door while the cake is baking for at least 50 minutes, since this *Kuchen* is very sensitive to drafts.

Like all members of the *Rührkuchen* family, *Sandkuchen* freezes well, and if tightly wrapped, keeps fresh for a few days. Here are my three favorite recipes.

Sandkuchen I

For years now, whenever our family goes on a car trip, we take along this cake. Since it is usually eaten an hour after we've set out, I have learned to bake two and hide one for later! This version is light as a spongecake, but the small amount of added butter helps it to stay moist for days.

Preheat oven to 375°F.
9 x 5 x 3-inch loaf pan   Line the pan with lightly buttered foil.

BATTER

4 tablespoons unsalted butter 1 cup sugar 5 eggs	Cream butter, sugar and eggs, using one of the methods on pages 11-13.

1 teaspoon vanilla extract
   Or
1 tablespoon rum
   Or
grated peel of 1 lemon
pinch of salt
	Add flavoring and salt.

1½ cups sifted flour 1 teaspoon baking powder	Fold in flour and baking powder.

Pour immediately into the prepared pan and bake on the lowest rack of a preheated 375°F oven for 50 to 60 minutes, or until a cake tester inserted in the center comes out clean. Let the cake cool in the pan for 10 minutes before turning out onto a cake rack to cool thoroughly.

Sandkuchen II

Increasing the amount of cornstarch in a *Sandkuchen* tends to increase the crumbliness of the cake. Cornstarch can give a lovely and delicate feeling to the cake, but one must be careful not to overdo it: the result may be too dry. This recipe lies between the spongy quality of No. I and the richness of No. III.

Preheat oven to 375°F.
9 x 5 x 3-inch loaf pan   Line the pan with lightly buttered foil.

                    BATTER

½ cup (1 stick) unsalted butter Cream butter, sugar, and egg yolks, using one of the methods on pages 11-13.
1 cup sugar
5 egg yolks
1 tablespoon rum   Add flavoring and salt
½ teaspoon vanilla extract
   Or
grated peel of ½ lemon
pinch of salt
1½ cups sifted flour   Fold in flour and cornstarch.
½ cup sifted cornstarch
5 egg whites   Beat egg whites separately and fold in gently.

Pour immediately into the prepared pan and bake on the lowest rack of a preheated 375°F oven for 60 minutes, or until a cake tester inserted in the middle comes out clean. Cool in the pan for 10 minutes before turning out onto a cake rack to cool thoroughly.

Sandkuchen III

Here we have the German equivalent of pound cake. It is a rich, pleasantly flavored cake that simply disintegrates on your tongue.

Preheat oven to 375°F.
10 x 5 x 3-inch loaf pan   Line the pan with lightly buttered foil.

                    BATTER

1 cup plus 2 tablespoons unsalted butter Cream butter, sugar, and egg yolks, using one of the methods on pages 11-13.
1¼ cups sugar
5 egg yolks
1 tablespoon rum   Add rum and vanilla, or lemon peel, and salt.
½ teaspoon vanilla extract
   Or
grated peel of ½ lemon
pinch of salt
2 cups sifted flour   Fold in flour and cornstarch.
¼ cup sifted cornstarch
5 egg whites   Beat egg whites separately and fold in delicately.

Pour immediately into the prepared pan and bake on the lowest rack of a preheated 375°F oven for 60 to 70 minutes, or until a cake tester inserted in the middle comes out clean. Cool in the pan for 10 minutes before turning out onto a cake rack to cool thoroughly.

Obstkuchen und flache Kuchen

(tarts)

When you look in the window of a German *Konditorei* or *Bäckerei* you can practically tell the season by the fruit tarts: fresh rhubarb and strawberry tarts in spring, apple and grape in autumn. And the pastry usually cradling these natural wonders is *Mürbteig,* which I prefer to translate as "rich tart pastry."

There are two basic ways of making tarts. Either the fresh fruit is baked together with the pastry shell, or the shell is completely prebaked and then filled with fresh, frozen, or canned fruits. A simple *Obstkuchen* is merely fruit baked with some raisins, nuts, and butter; and it takes only a little more time to be fancier with a soufflé topping or custard filling. With few exceptions, German tarts are open-faced.

Tarts are very easy to make and do not have to be time-consuming. You can do much of the work ahead of time, thanks to the freezer and refrigerator, by accomplishing a step here and there when you have a minute. Unless otherwise indicated, tarts can be baked a day ahead and stored in a cool place or in the refrigerator. A fully baked shell can be baked in advance and kept up to three days if tightly wrapped.

Other doughs, such as *Blätterteig* (puff pastry), are sometimes used for tart shells. *Hefeteig* (yeast dough) is often preferred in home baking by people who must limit their butter intake.

All tarts can be decorated with *Schlagsahne* (whipped cream) before serving. In the home, when *Obstkuchen* are served after a good meal or for afternoon coffee, one usually passes a bowl of lightly sweetened whipped cream around the table.

Mürbteig (rich tart pastry)

The word *Mürbteig* variously implies "mellow," "tender," "crisp," and "brittle": you will meet each of these qualities in the course of making and baking the dough. There are many variations on *Mürbteig,* depending on the relative proportions of butter, sugar, and flour or upon the addition of a special ingredient such as ground almonds, hard-cooked egg yolks, or cream.

Butter is so important in *Mürbteig* that the old name for it was *Süsser Butterteig* (sweet butter dough). Basically it is a first-class cookie dough, tender and crisp with a fine butter flavor. Certainly the variety of *Mürbteig* doughs coupled with the enormous range of fillings constitutes one of Germany's finest contributions to baking and gastronomy.

Mürbteig Recipes (rich tart pastry)

All recipes are meant for a 10-inch springform pan.

When several alternatives are given for the flavoring, see the individual tart recipes for which one to use.

Note that flour for rich tart pastry does not need to be sifted. Measurements given are for unsifted flour.

Guter Mürbteig (Rich Tart Pastry No. 1)

Here is a good choice for an unobtrusive crust; use it when the filling is delicately flavored and you do not want to overpower it. It is crisp, medium-sweet, and has the typical *Mürbteig* taste.

1¾ cups unbleached flour
⅓ cup sugar
1 egg or 2 egg yolks
½ cup plus 2 tablespoons
 unsalted butter
1 tablespoon heavy cream

pinch of salt
1 teaspoon vanilla extract
Or
grated peel of ½ lemon
Or
1 tablespoon dark rum

Feiner Mürbteig (Rich Tart Pastry No. 2)

A cookie-like crust, whose special crispness is due to a greater proportion of sugar. It goes well with all fruits and fillings.

1¾ cups unbleached flour
½ cup plus 1 tablespoon sugar
1 egg
½ cup plus 1 tablespoon
 unsalted butter

pinch of salt
grated peel of 1 lemon
Or
1½ teaspoons vanilla extract

Feinster Mürbteig (Rich Tart Pastry No. 3)

This is an especially fine crust and does honor to the literal translation of *Mürbteig*: "mellow dough." The crust has a nice yellow color and is sweet and crisp. Just delicious!

1¾ cups unbleached flour
½ cup sugar
3 egg yolks
½ cup plus 3 tablespoons
 unsalted butter
pinch of salt

1 teaspoon vanilla extract
Or
grated peel of 1 lemon
Or
1 teaspoon dark rum

Wiener Mürbteig (Rich Tart Pastry No. 4)

Four egg yolks give this *Mürbteig* a smooth, luxurious taste. It goes very well with a sweet filling.

1¾ cups unbleached flour
⅓ cup sugar
4 egg yolks
½ cup plus 2 tablespoons
    unsalted butter

pinch of salt
1 tablespoon lemon juice
1 teaspoon vanilla extract
    Or
grated peel of 1 lemon.

Schwäbischer Mürbteig (Rich Tart Pastry No. 5)

When this crust melts in your mouth you will forget the trouble it took to get four hard-cooked egg yolks through a fine sieve. I especially recommend it for a fully prebaked tart shell to be filled with custard and fruit.

2 cups unbleached flour
½ cup sugar
4 hard-cooked egg yolks
¾ cup unsalted butter
1 tablespoon dark rum
    Or
grated peel of 1 lemon
    Or
2 teaspoons vanilla extract

Boil eggs for 10 minutes.
Let cool. Rub the yolks through a fine sieve.

Mürbteig mit Ei und Backpulver (Rich Tart Pastry No. 6)

This light crust with baking powder has a neutral taste and is good for all kinds of tarts, especially the *Käsekuchen* (Cheese Tart).

1½ cups unbleached flour
½ cup cornstarch
1 teaspoon baking powder
⅓ cup sugar
1 egg

½ cup plus 2 tablespoons
    unsalted butter
pinch of salt
grated peel of 1 lemon
juice of ½ lemon

Einfacher Mürbteig (Rich Tart Pastry No. 7)

The simplest of these crusts has a low butter content, so baking powder is needed to make the pastry lighter. The taste is pleasant and the shell is quite good for a simple tart.

1¾ cups unbleached flour
1 teaspoon baking powder
⅓ cup sugar
1 egg
¼ cup (4 tablespoons)
    unsalted butter
3 tablespoons whole milk

pinch of salt
1½ teaspoons vanilla extract
    Or
1 tablespoon dark rum
    Or
grated peel of 1 lemon

Obstkuchen und Flache Kuchen

Mürbteig ohne Ei (Rich Tart Pastry No. 8)

If you choose to make a rich, custardy filling with lots of eggs, perhaps you would like to balance it with an eggless *Mürbteig* such as this one. It makes a very good tart shell, medium-sweet and very crisp.

1½ cups unbleached flour
⅓ cup sugar
½ cup plus 3 tablespoons
    unsalted butter
1½ teaspoons vanilla extract
    Or
1 tablespoon dark rum

Note: Because there is no egg to help bind the dough, it will take a little longer for the dough to form into a ball. Repeatedly compress the dough in the palms of your hands and release it.

Mandelmürbteig (Rich Tart Pastry No. 9)

This is a very crisp sugar crust. It is medium-sweet with a full, almond flavor. Because of the dryness of ground nuts and because there is no egg, this crust can be hard to roll out in one piece. I recommend doing the bottom of the pan first and then rolling out the sides separately. A good choice for a fully prebaked shell.

¾ cup unbleached flour
½ cup cornstarch
⅓ cup sugar
½ cup unsalted butter
¾ cup blanched, finely
    ground almonds
1 teaspoon vanilla extract
    Or
½ teaspoon almond extract

See Note to *Mürbteig* No. 8.

Note: Watch this crust carefully as it bakes. It should only brown very slightly; otherwise the almonds produce a bitter flavor.

Directions for Making Mürbteig, or Rich Tart Pastry
Method I: By Hand

Pastry-making is easy if you have all of the ingredients ready and work systematically. The mixing should go rapidly so that the butter will not soften appreciably.

Choose a large, smooth working surface such as wood, Formica, or marble. Have the butter and eggs chilled. If your recipe calls for baking powder, mix it together with the flour.

I like to make the pastry in a way that is pretty as well as efficient. This way of assembling ingredients also makes it easy to see what you have forgotten. Pour the flour on to the working surface. Make a well in the center (rather like a little volcano). Put the sugar into the well and tamp it down again into a well. On top of the sugar add eggs or egg yolks. Cut the chilled butter into one-inch pieces and place them evenly around the slopes of the well. Add flavorings (vanilla, lemon peel, rum) to the well.

Begin blending the pastry with a large unserrated knife such as a butcher knife or a pastry blender (I prefer a knife to a pastry blender). In this way the dough has less contact with warm hands and remains manageable. Start in the center, cutting the eggs into the sugar, and gradually work in the butter and flour. As you work, keep the ingredients together by scraping toward the center. When the dough forms it will first be mealy, like oatmeal, and then will begin to clump into pea-sized bits. When it starts to form larger lumps discard the knife and press the dough into a ball with your hands. Knead it with the heel of your hand for a minute or so, until the dough is thoroughly mixed. The dough should not be sticky. Gather the dough into a ball again and wrap in wax paper. Allow it to firm at least two hours in the refrigerator or one hour in the freezer.

Note: Rich Tart Pastry will keep about three to four days in the refrigerator, or you may freeze it for weeks. To keep it longer than a few hours, wrap plastic over the wax paper.

Method II: Heavy-Duty Mixer

A portable mixer is too light to work the stiff *Mürbteig*, but by all means use a heavy-duty machine with a flat beater attachment if you have one available. Arrange the ingredients in the bowl of the mixer just as described in Method I for a flat surface. Put the machine on its lowest setting to keep the flour from spraying out of the bowl.

Switch the machine on and off quickly a few times to moisten the flour, then let it run on a slow setting. The dough will go through the same stages as when it is worked by hand: mealy at first, followed by increasingly larger lumps. It is finished when the sides of the bowl are clean and the pastry is in a ball around the beater. Take it off and press it into a smooth ball. Wrap it in wax paper and chill for two hours in the refrigerator or for one hour in the freezing compartment.

See the note in Method I for making Rich Tart Pastry ahead of time.

Rolling and Shaping the Dough

Because of its high butter content, *Mürbteig* should be rolled out quickly, before the dough gets sticky. If it does become hard to handle, place it back in the refrigerator for a while. I find the following technique easiest:

Sprinkle your working surface very lightly with water. Smooth two pieces of wax paper, each about 1½ feet long, over the moist surface so that they overlap an inch or so. A little water will keep the wax paper from slipping as you roll, but too much will soak the paper and make it tear. Flour the paper lightly. Knead the chilled pastry with your knuckles until it is in a fairly flat circle. If it is too hard, hit it several times with the rolling pin to soften it. Flour the rolling pin and roll evenly in all directions, keeping the dough circular. Renew the light flour coating on the rolling pin occasionally if you need to, keeping in mind that too much flour will obscure the fine flavor of your pastry. Check your progress by setting the springform pan on the pastry. Depending on the height of the pan, the rolled-out dough should be about 2½ inches wider all around than the pan bottom. Continue rolling until the circle is about one-eighth inch thick in the center, which will be the bottom of the tart shell. Since the sides of the shell will brown somewhat faster than the bottom, the outer edges of the circle (which will form the sides) should be left a bit thicker to compensate for this. If the pastry does not form an even circle, trim the edges and patch by pressing the trimmed scraps into the gaps. When the dough is finished, transfer immediately to the pan.

Note: The pastry also can be rolled out directly onto a cold, floured surface, such as marble. If you do this, lift and turn the pastry occasionally during rolling so that it will not stick.

Lining the Pan

There is no need to butter or flour the pan—the pastry is so rich that it butters the pan as it bakes. I have found the following method helpful for moving pastry dough without breaking it:

Once the pastry has been rolled out on wax paper, lay another piece of wax paper on top of it. Hold the edge of the bottom paper and begin peeling it off as you roll the dough up into a cylinder. Peel carefully, but do not worry if the pastry cracks a little as it is being rolled up; you can fix it in the pan. (If the dough is hopelessly stuck to the paper, this indicates it has been rolled too long or is too warm: return it to the refrigerator until firm.) When you finish, the dough will be rolled around the top piece of wax paper and the bottom piece will have been peeled off. Turn the roll around, holding it over the pan. Unroll it so that the wax paper is on top and the pastry drops right into the pan as you unroll.

Pat the pastry into place with your fingers, smoothing out creases and working excess dough up toward the rim of the pan. Cut off the uneven edges just below the rim of the pan and use the scraps to patch thin places in the sides. If you wish, you can scallop the edges with a pastry wheel.

Note: If the dough is very fragile, you may want to roll out a small round for the bottom and then roll out a long strip for the sides separately. Combine the dough with your fingers.

Leftover dough may be wrapped securely in plastic and frozen. Later it can be turned into cookies or individual small fruit tarts.

Never let an unbaked tart shell stand in a warm room prior to placing it in the oven. If it has to wait, put it into the refrigerator.

Baking the Tart Shell

Now your *Mürbteig* is ready to bake. Preheat the oven to 400°F. If the recipe does not recommend prebaking, slip it into the refrigerator while preparing the filling. However, most of the recipes call for prebaking to avoid soggy crusts.

If it is to be either partially or fully baked before filling, it needs to be weighted down. Otherwise the sides will slip down and air pockets will form in the bottom. Here is how to weight it: generously butter a piece of lightweight foil or baking parchment and fit it into the tart shell, buttered side down. Press it against the sides. Fill with dry beans or pebbles (they can be kept on hand and used repeatedly). These hold the pastry against the pan during baking.

Bake on the lowest rack of the preheated oven for 10 to 12 minutes, or until the sides of the shell turn light gold (not brown). Let the shell cool a few minutes, then pour out the beans. Carefully strip off the foil. The bottom of the tart shell will look slightly moist.

For a *partially baked* shell, return to the oven for another 3 to 5 minutes, or until the wet look disappears and the shell looks "set."

For a *fully baked* shell, return to the oven for 10 to 15 minutes, or until the crust is lightly browned.

Note: Those rich tart pastry recipes with a high sugar content should be watched extra carefully because they brown rapidly.

Unmolding Tarts

When your tart is golden-brown and you have tested the filling, take it out of the oven and let it sit for 10 minutes. Take a big, smooth knife and run it around the sides of the pan to loosen the pastry completely. Now take the rim off your springform pan and let the steam escape for another 10 minutes. Loosen the bottom of the tart with your knife: push the knife between pastry and pan bottom as far as you can, keeping it flat so as not to cut into the tart, and turn the pan as you move the knife until the pastry does not stick on the bottom anywhere.

Have your cake rack ready. Taking the tart with pan bottom in one hand (with pot holder), slip the knife under the opposite side of the tart to give a start in slipping it over the raised edge of the bottom. Holding your tart level with the cake rack and balanced on one hand, give a fast jerk toward the rack. The tart should slip easily onto the rack. If you start to shift the tart to the rack and it appears too soft to slide without breaking, wait until it has cooled further before trying again.

Let the tart cool completely on the cake rack before transferring it to a serving plate. Then it will be easy just to tilt the rack and slide it onto the plate.

When Things Go Wrong

If you prebake the pastry shell before filling, you probably will not have any problem with a soggy crust. However, should it happen, here are some suggestions:

- Make certain your oven is reaching the correct temperature. You may have to check the dial setting with an oven thermometer.

- If your oven is like my old gas oven, you will want to use the lowest rack. I have found this helps the bottom crust to bake before the fruit gives up its juice.
- To help absorb part of the fruit juice, spread finely ground nuts, such as almonds or filberts, or fresh, good quality bread crumbs in the pastry shell before filling it.

If you have partially baked a pastry shell and the sides have browned a bit too much, it may be advisable to drape several 5-inch-wide strips of aluminum foil loosely around the edge of the pan before doing the final baking to prevent burning. This is only necessary with a topping (such as nut or streusel) which does not come up to the edge of the sides. You need not worry about a pastry shell filled with a meringue or soufflé topping, because this will puff up to the edge of the shell, thus preventing the sides from browning rapidly.

Rhabarberkuchen (rhubarb tart)

Even people who do not like rhubarb are delighted with this tart. The sweet, custardlike topping blends with the piquant fruit to form a special flavor.

Preheat oven to 400°F.

10-inch partially baked pastry shell, pages 31-37.	I recommend rich tart pastry No. 3 or No. 9. Flavor with vanilla or rum.
1½ pounds rhubarb (about 4 cups cleaned), fresh or frozen 2 tablespoons sugar	Wash rhubarb, remove woody ends, and cut into half-inch lengths. Toss with the sugar in a bowl and let stand for an hour. The sugar will dissolve and the rhubarb will give up juice. Drain in a colander and save the juice.
½ cup finely ground filberts, almonds, or fresh bread crumbs	Spread evenly over the bottom of the tart shell after it has been partially baked.

FILLING

4 egg yolks 1 cup sugar 1 tablespoon rhubarb juice	Beat egg yolks until smooth. Add sugar by spoonfuls and rhubarb juice. Continue beating until the mixture is pale yellow and fluffy.
2 teaspoons vanilla extract 4 tablespoons cornstarch	Add vanilla, mix in cornstarch, and set aside.
4 egg whites	In a separate bowl beat the egg whites until they form stiff peaks. Stir drained rhubarb into the egg yolk mixture. Delicately fold in the egg whites.

Pour the filling immediately into the partially baked shell and place the tart on the lowest rack of a preheated 400°F oven for 35 to 45 minutes, or until the shell and the filling are nicely browned. Check after 20 minutes to see if the top is browning too fast. If necessary place a piece of aluminum foil lightly on the top of the pan.

Cool in the pan for 10 minutes. Unbuckle the rim of the pan and wait another 10 minutes before unmolding it onto a cake rack to cool thoroughly. (See unmolding tarts, page 37.)

Serving Suggestions. Dust lightly with confectioners sugar or serve with *Schlagsahne* (whipped cream).

Rhabarberkuchen mit Haselnüssen
(rhubarb tart with filberts)

Perhaps a better name for this tart would be Filbert Tart with Rhubarb, since it contains three cups of ground nuts. Gooseberries are also an excellent fruit to use.

Preheat oven to 400°F.

10-inch partially baked pastry shell, pages 31-37.	Choose from any of the rich tart pastry recipes. Flavor with vanilla or rum.
2 pounds rhubarb (about 5 cups cleaned), fresh or frozen 3 tablespoons sugar	Wash rhubarb, remove woody ends, and cut into half-inch lengths. Toss in a bowl with the sugar and let stand an hour. The sugar will dissolve and the rhubarb will give up juice. Drain in a colander and save the juice.
3 cups finely ground filberts	Spread one cup of nuts in the bottom of the partially baked shell. Save the other two cups for the filling.

FILLING

3 egg yolks 1 cup sugar 1 tablespoon dark rum 2 tablespoons rhubarb juice	Beat egg yolks until smooth. Add sugar slowly by spoonfuls. Continue beating until the mixture is pale yellow and fluffy. Add rum and juice.
reserved 2 cups of filberts	Fold in filberts. The mixture will be quite thick.
3 egg whites	In a separate bowl beat the egg whites until they form stiff peaks. Mix drained fruit into the filling. Delicately fold in egg whites last.

Pour the filling immediately over the nuts in the partially baked shell, and bake the tart on the lowest rack of a preheated 400°F oven for 45

Obstkuchen und Flache Kuchen

minutes, or until the top of the filling is nicely browned. Check after 20 minutes to see if the top is browning too fast. If necessary place a piece of aluminum foil lightly on the top of the pan.

Cool in the pan for 10 minutes. Loosen the rim of the pan and wait another 10 minutes before unmolding it onto a cake rack to cool thoroughly. (See unmolding tarts, page 37.)

Einfacher Kirschenkuchen (simple cherry tart)

A rustic tart whose substantial filling consists of cherries and delicately flavored farina pudding. A perfect *Kuchen* for hungry guests!

Preheat oven to 400°F.

10-inch partially baked pastry shell, pages 31-37.	Choose from any of the rich tart pastry recipes. Flavor with vanilla or grated lemon peel.
1½ pounds sweet or sour cherries, pitted or unpitted, fresh, frozen, or canned (about 4 cups)	If the cherries are frozen, defrost completely. Drain cherries in a colander. Pat with paper towels so that they are as dry as possible. Set aside.

FARINA PUDDING

2 cups whole milk ¾ cup farina ¾ cup sugar	Place milk, farina, and sugar in a heavy saucepan and stir to blend with a wire whip. Bring to a boil, stirring frequently. Reduce heat and simmer for 3 minutes, or until farina is cooked and pudding is very thick.
2 egg yolks 2 tablespoons unsalted butter ½ teaspoon baking powder ½ teaspoon cinnamon grated peel of 1 lemon	Remove from heat and stir in egg yolks, butter, baking powder, and flavorings.
4 egg whites	In a separate bowl beat egg whites until they form stiff peaks. Fold cherries into farina. Gently fold in egg whites.

Pour the filling immediately into the partially baked shell and bake the tart on the lowest rack of a preheated 400°F oven for 45 to 50 minutes, or until the top of the filling is nicely browned. Check the tart after 20 minutes. If the filling is browning too rapidly, place a piece of aluminum foil lightly on top of the pan.

Cool in the pan for 10 minutes. Unbuckle the rim of the springform pan and wait another 10 minutes before unmolding it onto a cake rack to cool thoroughly. (See unmolding tarts, page 37.)

Kirschenkuchen mit Baiserhaube (cherry meringue tart)

With all of the possible combinations of pastries and fillings for German tarts, it is important to think about balance and contrast in both flavor and texture before selecting your components. Here a crisp, sweet meringue topping is set off by one of the simpler pastry crusts, while almonds and a touch of almond extract encourage the natural flavor of the cherries.

Preheat oven to 400°F.

10-inch partially baked pastry shell, pages 31-37.	I recommend rich tart pastry recipes No. 1, 4, 6, or 7. Flavor with vanilla.
2 pounds pitted sweet or sour cherries, fresh, frozen, or canned (about 5½ cups)	Thaw frozen cherries completely. Drain frozen or canned cherries thoroughly and pat them dry with paper towels. Set aside.

MERINGUE

4 egg whites 1 cup sugar 1 teaspoon almond extract	Beat egg whites at low speed until foamy. Increase speed to high and slowly add sugar by spoonfuls. Add the almond extract. Continue beating until whites form stiff peaks.
1½ cups medium-ground blanched almonds	Fold in 1 cup of the almonds very gently with a spatula. Set the meringue aside.

Spread the remaining one-half cup of almonds in the tart shell, followed by the cherries. Pour the meringue over all.

Bake immediately on the lowest rack of a preheated 400°F oven for 30 to 40 minutes, or until the meringue is browned and a knife inserted in the center comes out clean. Check after 20 minutes to see if the meringue is browning too fast. If necessary place a piece of aluminum foil lightly on top of the tart.

Cool in the pan for 10 minutes. Unbuckle the rim of the springform pan and wait another 10 minutes before unmolding it onto a cake rack to cool thoroughly. (See unmolding tarts, page 37.)

Stachelbeerkuchen (gooseberry tart)

Do you have a gooseberry bush in your garden? If not, get acquainted with this fruit by trying this fine tart with canned berries.

Preheat oven to 400°F.

10-inch partially baked pastry shell, pages 31-37.	Choose from any of the rich tart pastry recipes. Flavor with vanilla.
1½ pounds (about 4 cups) fresh gooseberries Or 2-pound can of gooseberries	Wash or drain berries in a colander. Pat them dry with a towel. Set aside.

FILLING

4 egg yolks ½ cup sugar	Beat egg yolks with sugar until smooth, thick, and pale yellow.
2 tablespoons cornstarch ½ cup sour cream grated peel of ½ lemon	Add cornstarch, sour cream, and lemon peel.
½ cup medium-ground blanched almonds	Fold in the nuts.
4 egg whites	In a separate bowl, beat the egg whites until stiff. Mix berries with the egg yolk mixture. Delicately fold in the egg whites last.

Pour the filling immediately into the partially baked shell and bake the tart on the lowest rack of a preheated 400°F oven for 40 minutes, or until the top and sides are nicely browned. Check after 20 minutes to see if the top is browning too fast. If necessary, place a piece of aluminum foil lightly on top of the tart.

Cool in the pan for 10 minutes. Loosen the rim of the pan and wait another 10 minutes before removing it to a cake rack to cool thoroughly. (See unmolding tarts, page 37.)

Pfirsichkuchen (peach tart)

This peach or apricot tart receives a topping pleasantly reminiscent of marzipan (almond paste). I prefer serving this *Kuchen* right after it has cooled, while it is still very crisp.

Preheat oven to 400°F. 10-inch partially baked pastry shell, pages 31-37.	Choose from any of the rich tart pastry recipes. Flavor with vanilla.
About 2 pounds fresh, firm peaches or apricots	Drop the fruit in boiling water for 10 to 15 seconds. Peel, halve, and remove pits. Set aside.

ALMOND STREUSEL

1¼ cups finely ground, blanched almonds ½ cup sifted flour ½ cup sugar ½ cup unsalted, chilled butter 1 teaspoon almond extract	For making streusel, see page 149.

Place the halved peaches or apricots, domed side up, in the partially baked shell. Spread the streusel topping evenly over the fruit.

Bake immediately on the lowest rack of a preheated 400°F oven for 40 minutes, or until the topping is nicely browned. Cool in the pan for 10 minutes. Loosen the rim of the springform pan and wait another 10 minutes before unmolding it onto a cake rack to cool thoroughly. (See unmolding tarts, page 37.)

Linzer Torte

More a tart than a torte, this Austrian specialty takes its name from the city of Linz on the Danube River. It is very rich, being a crisp *Mürbteig* containing ground almonds and spices which is spread with raspberry jam. Serve in thin wedges.

PASTRY CRUST

1 cup (2 sticks) unsalted butter
1 cup sugar
2 egg yolks
2 cups unbleached flour
2⅓ cups finely ground unblanched almonds
½ teaspoon cinnamon
big pinch of cloves

See directons for making rich tart pastry on pages 34-37.

Preheat oven to 400°F.

ASSEMBLING THE LINZER TORTE

10-inch springform pan
2 egg whites, beaten to blend
1 to 1⅓ cups red or black raspberry jam

Reserve one-third of the pastry for the lattice crust. Refrigerate it while lining the pan with the remaining two-thirds.

From the remaining two-thirds cut off one-sixth and set aside. Roll out the rest to fit the bottom of the pan (see pages 35-36).

Form the reserved one-sixth of the dough into a long roll about one-fourth-inch thick and one-half-inch high. Brush egg white sparingly around the edge of the bottom crust in the pan. Set the roll of dough on top of it (the egg white acts as a glue) and press it slightly down into the bottom crust.

Spread the raspberry jam evenly into the pastry shell.

Roll out the refrigerated one-third of the dough and cut it into strips one-half-inch wide with a knife or pastry wheel. Crisscross the strips of pastry to form a lattice top. The strips can be picked up easily by slipping a knife blade under them lengthwise.

Brush the lattice top with the remaining egg white.

Bake immediately in the lower middle of a preheated 400°F oven for 45 to 50 minutes, or until the pastry is a golden brown. Do not overbake, or the almonds may produce a bitter taste.

Cool in the pan for 10 minutes. Unbuckle the sides of the pan and wait another 10 minutes before unmolding it onto a cake rack to cool thoroughly. (See unmolding tarts, page 37.)

Obstkuchen und Flache Kuchen

Aprikosenkuchen mit Biskuithaube
(apricot tart with spongecake topping)

Piquant apricots are nestled in one of the sweeter *Mürbteig* shells. With a spongecake batter poured over the fruit, it might be said to resemble an upside-down cake in a tart shell.

Preheat oven to 400°F.

10-inch partially baked pastry shell, pages 31–37.	I recommend rich tart pastry recipes No. 2 or No. 3. Flavor with lemon peel, rum, or vanilla.
½ cup finely ground, blanched almonds	Spread nuts evenly in the bottom of the partially baked shell.
2 pounds fresh, semiripe apricots, medium sized	Wash, stone, and halve the apricots. Set aside.

BATTER

3 egg whites ½ cup sugar pinch of salt 2 teaspoons lemon juice 1 teaspoon vanilla extract 3 egg yolks ⅔ cup sifted cake flour	Use Method I, page 64, for preparing the batter.

Arrange apricot halves over the ground almonds in a circular pattern, domed side up. Fill out spaces with smaller slices of apricot.

Pour the spongecake batter over the fruit.

Bake immediately on the lowest rack of a preheated 400°F oven for 45 minutes, or until a cake tester inserted in the middle comes out clean. Check the tart after 20 minutes to see if the top is browning too fast. If necessary place a piece of aluminum foil lightly across the top of the tart.

Cool in the pan for 10 minutes. Unbuckle the rim of the pan and wait another 10 minutes before unmolding it onto a wire rack to cool thoroughly. (See unmolding tarts, page 37.)

Serving Suggestion. Dust lightly with confectioners sugar.

Traubenkuchen (grape tart)

In German baking, grapes are often used fresh in an *Obsttorte* or are mixed with custard or whipped cream and placed in a fully baked tart shell. However, this old recipe calls for them to be baked along with the filling. The result is delicious.

Preheat oven to 400°F.

10-inch partially baked pastry shell, pages 31–37.	Choose from any of the rich tart pastry recipes. Flavor with vanilla.

2 pounds (about 6 cups) fresh seedless grapes	Remove stems and wash grapes. Drain in a colander. Set aside.

FILLING

4 egg yolks 1 cup sugar	Beat egg yolks until smooth. Add sugar by spoonfuls. Continue beating until the mixture is pale yellow and fluffy.
½ teaspoon almond extract Or 1 tablespoon kirsch	Add almond extract or kirsch.
2 tablespoons cornstarch ¾ cup medium-ground blanched almonds	Mix in cornstarch and nuts. Set aside.
4 egg whites	In a separate bowl, beat egg whites until stiff. Add the grapes to the egg-nut mixture. Delicately fold in the egg whites last.

Pour the filling immediately in the partially baked shell and bake the tart on the lowest rack of a preheated 400°F oven for 45 minutes, or until the top of the filling is nicely browned. Check after 20 minutes to see if the top is browning too fast. If necessary place a piece of aluminum foil lightly on the top of the pan.

Cool in the pan for 10 minutes. Loosen the rim of the springform pan and wait another 10 minutes before unmolding it onto a cake rack to cool thoroughly. (See unmolding tarts, page 37.)

Serving Suggestion. Dust lightly with confectioners sugar.

Heidelbeerkuchen (blueberry tart)

Those who dote on blueberry muffins and pies will find a new favorite here. Fresh blueberries are preferable because they seem to retain both their shape and their juices better; but if you can only obtain frozen ones, see the special note on frozen blueberries at the end of this recipe.

Preheat oven to 400°F.

10-inch partially baked pastry shell, pages 31-37.	Choose from any of the rich tart pastry recipes. Flavor with vanilla.
2 pounds (about 6 cups) blueberries	Wash and dry blueberries.
⅔ cup sugar 2 cups finely ground filberts or almonds 1½ teaspoons cinnamon	Mix sugar, nuts, and cinnamon together. Spread half of this mixture on the bottom of the partially baked shell. Place the blueberries in next, and cover them with the rest of the nut mixture.
2 tablespoons unsalted butter	Dot the tart with thin slices of butter.

Obstkuchen und Flache Kuchen

Bake immediately on the lowest rack of a preheated 400°F oven for 20 minutes, or until the sides of tart are lightly browned. Cool in the pan for 10 minutes. Unbuckle the sides of the springform pan and wait another 10 minutes before unmolding it onto a cake rack to cool thoroughly. (See unmolding tarts, page 37.)

Note: Frozen blueberries should be thawed completely. Because they tend to give up a lot of juice when baked, they are best used in a fully baked tart shell.

To use them in this recipe, proceed as follows. Place berries in a colander until they are completely thawed and are no longer dripping freely. Sprinkle 2 tablespoons cornstarch over them and mix with a spoon. Then proceed as above.

Käsekuchen (cheese tart)

The Queen of Tarts! Ever since cheesecake was brought to the New World by German and Austrian cooks, it has ranked among the favorites of the land. I think you will find the flavor and texture of this original German recipe a delightful change from the usual American version.

Preheat oven to 400°F.

10-inch springform pan, lined with rich tart pastry, pages 31-37.	Choose from any of the rich tart pastry recipes. Flavor with lemon peel or vanilla.
½ cup sultanas or raisins 1 teaspoon flour	Plump the sultanas in boiling water for one or two minutes. Drain, dry, and cool. Dust with flour and set aside.

CHEESE FILLING

4 egg yolks 1 cup sugar 3 cups *Quark,* pages 149-151 2 cups sour cream 3 tablespoons cornstarch 1 teaspoon vanilla extract grated peel of 1 lemon juice of ½ lemon	In a large mixing bowl, beat egg yolks until smooth. Add sugar by spoonfuls, beating until the mixture is pale yellow and fluffy. Continue to beat while slowly adding *Quark,* sour cream, cornstarch, and flavorings.
4 egg whites	In a separate bowl beat the egg whites until stiff. Fold gently into the *Quark*-egg mixture.

Remove the pastry-lined pan from the refrigerator and distribute the floured sultanas over the bottom. Pour in the filling. It should not be higher than the top of the pastry shell.

Place immediately on the lowest rack of a preheated 400°F oven for 60 to 70 minutes. The filling will puff and form a top crust similar to that of a soufflé.

After 45 minutes, carefully take the tart out of the oven and make one-inch slits with a knife at the side under the puffed top. This allows steam to escape, avoiding a very high tart which collapses upon cooling.

If the tart browns too fast, rest a piece of foil lightly on the top.

Cool in the pan for 10 minutes. Loosen the rim of the springform pan and wait 30 minutes before unmolding it onto a cake rack to cool thoroughly.

If the top of your filling is even with the edge of the pastry crust, you may unmold the *Käsekuchen* in the following way. Lightly butter a cake rack and lay it on top of the tart. With one hand on the rack and one under the tart, reverse it so that it is upside down on the rack. Loosen the bottom of the pan with the point of a knife and remove it. Leave the tart on the rack until it is cool. Then turn it right side up onto a serving plate.

If the edge of the pastry crust is higher than the filling, see page 37 for unmolding tarts.

Serving Suggestions. Sprinkle the *Käsekuchen* lightly with confectioners sugar, or serve with *Schlagsahne* (whipped cream).

Cheese Cherry Tart

Using the same method and proportions, substitute 1½ pounds pitted, sour or sweet cherries for the raisins. Make sure that cherries are well drained and dry before putting them in the bottom of the pastry shell.

Johannisbeerkuchen (red currant tart)

It is a pity that red currants are seldom seen in supermarkets anymore. If they suddenly appear, or if you are lucky enough to have your own red currant bushes, try this delicious tart.

Preheat oven to 400°F.

10-inch-partially baked pastry shell, pages 31-37.	Choose from any of the rich tart pastry recipes. Flavor with vanilla.
1½ pounds red currants (4½ cups without stems)	Remove stems and wash currants. Drain in a colander. Set aside.

MERINGUE

4 egg whites 1¼ cups sugar 1½ teaspoons vanilla extract	Beat egg whites on low speed until foamy. Increase speed to high and slowly add sugar by spoonfuls. Add the vanilla extract. Continue beating until whites form stiff peaks.
1 cup medium-fine-ground unblanched almonds	By hand, gently fold in the almonds. Fold in currants.

Obstkuchen und Flache Kuchen

Pour the meringue mixture into the partially baked shell.

Bake immediately on the lowest rack of a preheated 400°F oven for about 45 minutes. Check after 20 minutes to see if the top is browning too fast. If necessary place a piece of aluminum foil lightly on the top of the pan to prevent burning.

The tart is done when the meringue has set and both it and the pastry are browned. If you test the meringue with a knife it may still be moist in the center. This is perfectly fine. The berries give up so much juice during baking that the meringue will never be completely dry.

Cool in the pan for 10 minutes. Unbuckle the rim of the pan and wait another 10 minutes before unmolding it onto a cake rack to cool thoroughly. (See unmolding tarts, page 37.)

Pflaumenkuchen (plum tart)

You can use early plums for this refreshing tart—but be sure they are flavorful. Of the various varieties available, I have found that California Nubiana most resemble German summer plums.

Preheat oven to 400°F.

10-inch partially baked pastry shell, pages 31-37.	Choose from any of the rich tart pastry recipes. Increase the recipe by half. Refrigerate ⅓ of the dough for the lattice top while prebaking the shell and preparing the plums.
2 pounds fresh plums ¾ cup sugar	Wash, pit, and quarter the plums. Place in a heavy saucepan. Add the sugar and stir continuously until it comes to a boil.
2 tablespoons cornstarch 2 tablespoons water	Dissolve cornstarch in water and add to the plums. Let boil for 3 to 5 minutes or until the plums are tender but still hold their shape. This mixture should now be fairly thick.
2 tablespoons unsalted butter (optional)	Off heat, stir in the butter.
1 cup coarsely chopped walnuts or almonds	Add nuts. Set aside.

Lattice Top: Roll out the refrigerated one-third of the dough and cut it into strips one-half-inch wide with a knife or pastry wheel.

Pour the plum mixture into the partially baked shell. Crisscross it with strips of pastry to form a lattice top. The strips can be picked up easily by slipping a knife blade under them lengthwise.

Bake immediately on the lowest rack of a preheated 400°F oven for 30 minutes, or until the sides of the tart and lattice top are lightly browned.

Cool in the pan for 10 minutes. Unbuckle the rim of the pan and wait another 10 minutes before unmolding it onto a cake rack to cool thoroughly. (See unmolding tarts, page 37.)

Serving Suggestions. Dust lightly with confectioners sugar. Serve each piece with a spoonful of *Schlagsahne* (whipped cream).

Zwetschgenkuchen (prune plum tart)

Late-season, tart-tasting plums are called *Zwetschgen* in Germany. A similar, though milder, variety is available in North America under the name "prune plum." They usually turn up in the supermarkets around the first days of September. As a native Swabian, I am particularly partial to *Zwetschgenkuchen,* since it is a Swabian speciality. This attractive tart can be made either with a yeast dough or a *Mürbteig* base and has the traditional streusel topping.

Preheat oven to 425°F.

10-inch springform pan, lined with rich tart pastry, pages 31-37.	Choose from any of the rich tart pastry recipes. Flavor with vanilla or lemon peel. Refrigerate while preparing the plums and topping.
2½ pounds firm prune plums	Wash and dry plums. Slice down one side only of the plum and remove the stone. Set aside.
	Note: If your plums are very juicy, prebake the pastry shell before filling it. Adjust baking temperature to 400°F and bake the tart for only 30 to 35 minutes.
½ cup medium-ground blanched almonds or fresh bread crumbs	Spread nuts or bread crumbs in the pastry shell.

Open the plums like little books, and arrange them in the shell in concentric rings, standing upright, supporting each other. This allows you to pack them tightly into the pastry shell.

Master recipe for streusel, page 149	Spread the streusel topping evenly over the plums.

Bake immediately on the lowest rack of a preheated 425°F oven for 15 minutes. Then turn heat to 400°F and bake for 30 minutes more, or until the topping is golden brown.

Cool in the pan for 10 minutes. Unbuckle the rim of the pan and wait another 10 minutes before unmolding it onto a cake rack to cool thoroughly. (See unmolding tarts, page 37.)

Serving Suggestion. Serve each piece with a spoonful of *Schlagsahne* (whipped cream).

Birnenkuchen (pear tart)

Why have the culinary possibilities of the pear been so ignored in modern baking? You will wonder too when you taste this exceptionally pleasing, though unusual, tart which comes to me from my grandmother. It is an excellent *Kuchen* for an afternoon *Kaffeeklatsch,* but the fine combination of pears and almond-flavored soufflé also makes it suitable for an important dinner.

Preheat oven to 400°F.

10-inch partially baked pastry shell, pages 31-37.	Choose from any of the rich tart pastry recipes. Flavor with vanilla.
2 cups cold water 1 tablespoon lemon juice	Mix water and lemon juice in a bowl.
1½ to 2 pounds firm, ripe pears	Peel and halve the pears. Drop each half in the acidulated water to keep it from discoloring. Set aside.

SOUFFLÉ FILLING

4 egg yolks ½ cup sugar	Beat egg yolks until smooth. Add sugar gradually, beating until the mixture is pale yellow and fluffy.
1 cup sour cream	Mix in sour cream by spoonfuls.
1 tablespoon cornstarch ½ teaspoon almond extract	Add cornstarch and almond flavoring.
1 cup finely ground blanched almonds	Fold in the almonds.
4 egg whites	Beat the egg whites in a separate bowl until they form stiff peaks. Fold egg whites delicately into egg yolk mixture.

Dry the pears in a towel. Arrange them concentrically in the partially baked tart shell, filling the gaps with small pieces.

Pour the filling over the pears and bake immediately in a preheated 400°F oven on the lowest rack for 40 to 45 minutes, or until the filling has puffed and browned nicely. Check after 20 minutes to see if the top is browning too fast. If necessary place a piece of aluminum foil lightly on the top of the pan.

Cool in the pan for 10 minutes. Loosen the rim of the springform pan and wait another 10 minutes before unmolding it onto a cake rack to cool thoroughly. (See unmolding tarts, page 37.)

Apfelkuchen mit Guss
(apple tart with soufflé filling)

Here is one of the classic apple tarts of Swabia, in southwestern Germany. Sliced apples are covered with a refreshing filling of sour cream, eggs, and lemon peel which has an airy lightness similar to a soufflé.

Preheat oven to 400°F.

10-inch springform pan, lined with rich tart pastry, pages 31-37.	Choose from any of the rich tart pastry recipes. Flavor with vanilla or lemon peel. Refrigerate while preparing the apples.
2 pounds tart, crisp, medium-sized apples	On how to prepare apples for tarts, see page 9. Toss with lemon juice and sugar. Set aside.
1 tablespoon lemon juice	*Note:* If the apples are very juicy, prebake the pastry shell before filling it; but then subtract 10 minutes from the final baking.
1 tablespoon sugar	

Arrange the apples on the pastry so that they overlap slightly and form concentric circles. Do not press them down into the pastry.

Bake in a preheated 400°F oven on the lowest rack for about 20 minutes, or until the crust is slightly browned.

While the shell (with apples) bakes, prepare the filling.

SOUFFLÉ FILLING

4 egg yolks	Beat egg yolks until smooth. Add sugar gradually, beating until the mixture is pale yellow and fluffy.
½ cup sugar	
¾ cup sour cream	Mix in cream by spoonfuls.
3 tablespoons cornstarch grated peel of 1 lemon	Add cornstarch and lemon peel. Set aside.
4 egg whites	Beat the egg whites in a separate bowl with sugar until they form stiff peaks. Fold egg whites delicately into egg yolk mixture.
1 tablespoon sugar	

Remove the pan from the oven and pour the soufflé over the apples. The filling should not go higher than the edge of the pastry.

Return to the oven for 30 minutes, or until the filling has puffed and browned nicely. If the tart browns too fast, place a piece of aluminum foil lightly on the top of the pan to prevent burning.

Cool in the pan for 10 minutes. Unbuckle the sides of the springform pan and wait another 10 minutes before unmolding it onto a cake rack to cool thoroughly. (See unmolding tarts, page 37.)

Variation. Add ½ cup of medium-fine blanched almonds or filberts to the filling.

Quark-Apfelkuchen (quark apple tart)

As a student I frequented an old, *gemütliches* cafe just to eat this *Kuchen*. In fact, I even used to skip a midday meal to be able to enjoy this treat. Here is my own re-creation of it.

Preheat oven to 400°F.
10-inch partially baked pastry shell, pages 31-37.
1½ pounds crisp, tart, medium-sized apples
2 teaspoons sugar
2 teaspoons lemon juice

Choose from any of the rich tart pastry recipes. Flavor with lemon peel.
On how to prepare apples for tarts, see page 9. Toss with lemon juice and sugar. Set aside.

QUARK FILLING

2 cups *Quark,* page 149.
2 egg yolks
½ cup sugar

Beat *Quark* until smooth. Mix in egg yolks. Add sugar, a spoonful at a time, and continue beating until the sugar crystals are dissolved and the mixture looks light and fluffy.

2 tablespoons cornstarch
grated peel of ½ lemon
½ teaspoon vanilla extract
 Or
1 tablespoon dark rum
½ cup currants (if you wish, soak several hours in rum)

Mix in cornstarch. Add flavoring.

Fold in currants by hand.
 Note: The mixture should be fairly thick. If for some reason it is not, add 1 more tablespoon of cornstarch.

Pour the filling in the partially baked shell and even out with a spatula. Arrange the apple slices, slightly overlapping, in two concentric circles. To give the apples a shine, sprinkle a pinch of sugar on each one, being careful not to sugar the *Quark* mixture.

Bake immediately on the lowest rack of a preheated 400°F oven for 45 to 50 minutes, or until the filling appears thickened.

Cool in the pan for 10 minutes. Unbuckle the rim of the springform pan and wait another 10 minutes before unmolding it onto a cake rack to cool thoroughly. (See unmolding tarts, page 37.)

Apfelkuchen mit Geleeguss (glazed apple tart)

A simple tart to make, and yet the sparkling glaze gives it a professional look. You can decorate further with slivered almonds and rosettes of whipped cream.

Preheat oven to 400°F.
10-inch springform pan, lined with rich tart pastry, pages 31-37.
2 pounds tart, crisp, medium-sized apples
1 tablespoon lemon juice
1 tablespoon sugar

Choose from any of the rich tart pastry recipes. Flavor with rum. Refrigerate while preparing the apples.

On how to prepare apples for tarts, see page 9. Toss with lemon juice and sugar. *Note:* If the apples are very juicy, prebake the pastry shell before filling it; but subtract 10 to 15 minutes from final baking.

¼ cup blanched almonds or filberts, ground medium-fine 1 tablespoon sugar	Mix nuts and sugar.

Arrange the apple slices in the pastry-lined pan so that they overlap slightly and form two concentric circles. Sprinkle them with the nut-sugar mixture and bake the tart on the lowest rack of a preheated 400°F oven for 35 to 40 minutes, or until the sides of the pastry are golden brown and the apples are tender.

Cool in the pan for 10 minutes. Unbuckle the sides of the pan and wait another 10 minutes before unmolding it onto a cake rack to cool thoroughly. (See unmolding tarts, page 37.) When the tart is completely cool, transfer it to a serving platter and add the glaze.

Red currant glaze, page 167 (or apple glaze)	Pour immediately over the tart and let cool.
¼ cup blanched, slivered almonds (optional)	Decorate the tart with slivered almonds.

Apfelkuchen mit Schaumguss (cloud-top apple tart)

The meringue topping which gives this tart its distinctiveness is a good way to use up that little bowl of egg whites cluttering up your refrigerator or freezer. Flavor it with rum or lemon juice. If you do not have apples, it is good on any other fruit tart as well.

Preheat oven to 400°F.	
10-inch springform pan, lined with rich tart pastry, pages 31-37.	Choose from any of the rich tart pastry recipes. Flavor with lemon peel. Refrigerate while preparing the apples.
2 pounds tart, crisp, medium-sized apples 1 tablespoon lemon juice 1 tablespoon sugar	On how to prepare apples for tarts, see page 9. Toss with lemon juice and sugar. *Note:* If the apples are very juicy, prebake the pastry shell before filling it; but then subtract 10 to 15 minutes from the final baking.
½ cup currants (optional)	Plump the currants in boiling water for one or two minutes. Leave in a colander to drain and cool. Or soak currants in rum for several hours.
1 cup blanched almonds, ground medium fine	Set aside ½ cup for the meringue topping.

Spread the remaining ½ cup of ground almonds in the bottom of the pastry-lined pan. Arrange the apple slices over them so that they overlap slightly and form concentric circles. Distribute currants between the slices.

Obstkuchen und Flache Kuchen

Bake immediately on the lowest rack of a preheated 400°F oven for 30 minutes, or until the apples are tender and the pastry is lightly browned. While the shell with fruit is prebaking, prepare the meringue.

MERINGUE TOPPING

5 egg whites 1 cup sugar 2 tablespoons lemon juice grated peel of ½ lemon Or 1 tablespoon dark rum	Beat the egg whites with sugar until they form stiff peaks. Add lemon juice and peel, or rum.
reserved ½ cup of ground almonds	Delicately fold in ground almonds.

Pour the egg white mixture over the partially baked tart at once and return to the oven for about 15 minutes. It is done when the meringue is lightly browned and a knife blade inserted into the center comes out clean.

Cool in the pan for 10 minutes. Unbuckle the sides of the pan and wait another 10 minutes before unmolding it onto a cake rack to cool thoroughly. (See unmolding tarts, page 37.)

Alt Wiener Apfelkuchen (Old Vienna apple tart)

Austrians have always loved jam-filled tarts and cakes, and this apricot and almond filled apple tart is one of their best. The upper crust bakes down over apple halves, leaving a lovely pattern of little golden domes.

Preheat oven to 400°F.

10-inch partially baked pastry shell, pages 31-37.	Choose from any of the rich tart pastry recipes and increase the amount by one half. Flavor with lemon peel or rum. Refrigerate ⅓ of the dough for the upper crust while prebaking the shell and preparing the apples.
1½ pounds tart, crisp, small-sized apples	Peel, halve, and core the apples, extracting with the core enough of the apple to leave a large cavity for the filling.
1 tablespoon lemon juice	Toss apples with lemon juice. Set aside.
1½ cups finely ground blanched almonds 6 tablespoons apricot preserves ⅛ teaspoon almond extract	Mix almonds, preserves, and almond extract together to form a thick paste.
½ cup raisins	Plump the raisins in boiling water for one or two minutes and let drain in a colander. Or soak raisins in rum for several hours.

54   Obstkuchen und Flache Kuchen

törtchen (Fruit Tartlets)

Marmorkuchen (Marble Cake) and *Orangenkuchen* (Orange Cake)

Fill the apple halves with the nut-preserves mixture. Domed side up, arrange apples in concentric circles in the shell. Fill out spaces between apples with raisins.

Roll out the reserved pastry dough for the upper crust. The layer should fit over the apples and should overlap the sides of the prebaked tart shell; otherwise the top edge of the sides may brown too much. Press the pastry down slightly over the apples so that the apple pattern shows through.

Bake immediately on the lowest rack of a preheated 400°F oven for 35 to 40 minutes, or until the upper crust is golden brown.

Cool in the pan for 10 minutes. Unbuckle the rim of the pan and wait another 10 minutes before unmolding it onto a cake rack to cool thoroughly. (See unmolding tarts, page 37.)

Apfelkuchen mit Nüssen (apple tart with nuts)

Layers of apples, nuts, and raisins are basted with melted butter in this easy-to-assemble tart. Although any kind of nut can be used, I find that walnuts give a rich, distinctive flavor.

Preheat oven to 400°F.

10-inch springform pan, lined with rich tart pastry, pages 31-37.	Choose from any of the rich tart pastry recipes. Flavor with vanilla or rum. Refrigerate while preparing the apples.
2 pounds tart, crisp, medium-sized apples 1 tablespoon lemon juice 1 tablespoon sugar	On how to prepare apples for tarts, see page 9. Toss with lemon juice and sugar. *Note:* If the apples are very juicy, prebake the pastry shell before filling it; but then subtract 10 to 15 minutes from the final baking.
1 cup raisins	Plump the raisins in boiling water for one or two minutes. Leave in a colander to drain and cool. Or soak raisins in rum for several hours.
1 teaspoon flour	Toss raisins with the flour and set aside.
1½ cups medium-ground walnuts, almonds, or filberts ⅓ cup sugar	Mix nuts with sugar. Set aside.
4 tablespoons unsalted butter, melted	

Spread one-half cup of the nut-sugar mixture over the bottom of the pastry-lined pan. Next sprinkle on the raisins. Arrange the apple slices, slightly overlapping, over the raisins in concentric circles. Distribute the rest of the nuts and sugar evenly over the apples. Dribble melted butter over all.

Bake immediately on the lowest rack of a preheated 400°F oven for 40 to 45 minutes, or until the sides of tart are lightly browned.

Cool in the pan for 10 minutes. Unbuckle the sides of the springform pan and wait another 10 minutes before unmolding it onto a cake rack to cool thoroughly. (See unmolding tarts, page 37.)

Apfelkuchen mit Brosamen (apple tart with bread crumbs)

Of all the apple tarts this is the simplest. My mother used to make it *zum gleich essen* (to eat right away) for Saturday afternoon coffee. The fancy one she made at the same time had to be saved for Sunday. Any other fruit can be substituted for the apples; especially good are plums, rhubarb, or blueberries.

10-inch springform pan, lined with rich tart pastry, pages 32-37.	Choose from any of the rich tart pastry recipes. Flavor with vanilla or lemon peel. Refrigerate while preparing the apples.
2 pounds crisp, tart, medium-sized apples	On how to prepare apples for tarts, see page 9. Toss apples with lemon juice, sugar, and cinnamon. *Note:* If the fruit is very juicy, prebake the pastry shell before filling it; but then subtract about 10 minutes from the final baking.
1 tablespoon lemon juice	
1 tablespoon sugar	
1 teaspoon cinnamon	

TOPPING

Preheat oven to 400°F.

¾ cup fresh bread crumbs Or ½ cup bread crumbs and ¼ cup finely ground filberts or almonds ⅓ cup sugar	Mix bread crumbs, nuts, and sugar together. Spread ¼ cup of this mixture in the bottom of the crust. Arrange the apple slices in concentric circles, overlapping them slightly. Sprinkle the rest of the topping over the apples.
2 tablespoons unsalted butter	Cut the butter into slivers and distribute it evenly over the topping.

Bake immediately on the lowest rack of a preheated 400°F oven for 35 minutes, or until the top and sides of the tart are nicely browned.

Cool in the pan for 10 minutes. Unbuckle the rim of the pan and wait another 10 minutes before unmolding it onto a cake rack to cool thoroughly. (See unmolding tarts, page 37.)

Erdbeer Krokant Kuchen (strawberry brittle tart)

A refreshing dessert for summertime, since it requires only a few minutes oven time for the shell and has a cool fruit filling. Everything can be done a day ahead (the *Krokant* months ahead, if frozen), except for folding the fruit into the whipped cream. It is also excellent made with blueberries or raspberries.

10-inch fully baked pastry shell, pages 31-37.	I recommend rich tart pastry No. 5 or No. 9. Flavor with vanilla.
1½ cups *Krokant* (toasted almond brittle), page 170.	Spread the *Krokant* evenly in the bottom of the baked tart shell.
2½ pounds (about 3 pints) fresh strawberries	Wash and hull strawberries. Drain in a colander Cut each berry into quarters. If you wish, reserve 9 whole, small berries with the hull on for decoration.
1 pint whipping cream	
3 tablespoons sugar	For directions on how to whip cream, see page 58. You may wish to add gelatin to assure sufficient thickness.
1 teaspoon vanilla extract Or	
1 tablespoon dark rum	

Not more than one hour before serving, fold strawberries into the whipped cream and spread the mixture over the *Krokant*.

Decorate with whole strawberries. I like one in the middle and one on each of the eight pieces which will be cut.

Refrigerate until serving.

Blueberry Brittle Tart

2 pounds (about 6 cups) fresh blueberries	Wash and drain blueberries. Flavor the whipped cream with 1 teaspoon almond extract. Reserve some *Krokant* for decoration.

Raspberry Brittle Tart

2 pounds (about 6 cups) fresh raspberries	Wash and drain raspberries. If you wish, reserve some for decoration. Flavor the whipped cream with 1½ teaspoons vanilla extract or 2 tablespoons cognac.

Apfelmuskuchen (hot or cold applesauce tart)

The rich, full taste of homemade applesauce and freshly whipped cream are set off to perfection here. Make this tart in apple season when you can't resist buying lots of apples or your apple tree is producing faster than you can eat. You can bake the tart shell and make the applesauce ahead of time, then put them together just before serving.

10-inch fully baked pastry shell, pages 31-37.	Choose from any of the rich tart pastry recipes. Especially recommended is No. 9. Flavor with vanilla or rum.
4 pounds tart, crisp apples ¾ cup sugar 1 stick of cinnamon (optional)	Peel, core, and thinly slice the apples. Combine apples, sugar, and cinnamon in a heavy saucepan. Cover and cook slowly for about 15 minutes, or until the apples are tender. Stir occasionally. Remove from heat and mash with a potato masher until you have thick applesauce. *Note:* The applesauce should be rough. Do not use a food mill or electric blender, since the applesauce produced will be too thin and will not hold its shape when the tart is cut. Commercial applesauce is entirely unsuitable.
1 tablespoon lemon juice 1 tablespoon dark rum 1 cup sultanas	Stir in lemon juice, rum, and raisins. Set aside to cool, or prepare the shell to be filled immediately if the tart is to be eaten warm.
½ pint whipping cream 2 teaspoons sugar 1 teaspoon rum	Whip cream until stiff. Add the rum.

Spread applesauce in the tart shell; if you wish, reserve about 4 tablespoons for decoration.

With a spatula, spread whipped cream over the applesauce. Place reserved applesauce in the center of the whipped cream.

Bayerischer Apfelkuchen (Bavarian apple tart)

This is truly a wonderful tart to look at: a fully baked pastry shell is filled with custard and tender, cooked apples and is then glazed.

10-inch fully baked pastry shell, pages 31-37.	I recommend rich tart pastry recipes No. 5 or No. 9. Flavor with vanilla.
2½ pounds tart, medium-sized apples 3 tablespoons sugar 1 cup water 2 tablespoons lemon juice	Peel, core and quarter the apples. In a heavy saucepan, bring water, sugar, and lemon juice to a boil. Drop the apples into the boiling liquid. Cover the pan and simmer 6 to 10 minutes, or until the apples are tender when pierced with a knife. *Note:* Apples must hold their shape. Do not overcook. With a slotted spoon remove apples to a rack to drain and cool. Save the apple syrup.
2 to 2½ cups custard filling, page 160, flavored with	Unmold the chilled custard into the pastry shell. Arrange the apple slices over it so that they

grated peel of 1 lemon and 1 teaspoon vanilla extract
Or
2 tablespoons dark rum

GLAZE

¾ cup reserved apple syrup
¾ cup apple, currant, or apricot jelly
¼ cup sugar

Combine apple syrup, jelly, and sugar in a heavy saucepan. Boil until the glaze coats a spoon lightly and the last drops to fall from the spoon are sticky and hold their shape. A candy thermometer will show 225° to 228°F. Pour hot glaze over the apples.

¼ cup blanched, slivered almonds (optional)

Decorate finished tart with a ring of nuts around the edge of the glaze.

Refrigerate the tart and serve within a few hours.
Serving Suggestion. Serve with *Schlagsahne* (whipped cream).
Variations. Use the same method, substituting pears. Or use fresh strawberries, blueberries, or raspberries. Frozen or canned fruits, such as apricots, peaches, cherries, and pineapple, are fine. A combination of them can be used to make a mixed fruit tart. Another idea is to alternate the fruit with slices of banana.
The gelatin glaze, page 167, also provides an interesting variation.

Rhabarberkuchen mit Geleeguss (glazed rhubarb tart)

A first cousin to the Bavarian apple tart, with a custard base and glazed topping. Since there are a few adjustments, here is the recipe again in full.

10-inch fully baked pastry shell, pages 31-37.

Choose from any of the rich tart pastry recipes. Flavor with vanilla.

1½ pounds rhubarb (about 4 cups cleaned)
¾ cup sugar

Wash rhubarb and discard woody ends. Cut into 1½ to 2-inch pieces. Combine rhubarb and sugar in a heavy saucepan. Cover and cook 3 to 5 minutes, or until the rhubarb is tender but keeps its shape. Remove rhubarb from its syrup with a slotted spoon. Reserve syrup. Drain rhubarb in a colander and let cool.

2 to 2½ cups custard filling, page 160, flavored with
2 teaspoons vanilla extract
Or
2 tablespoons rum
Or
½ cup finely ground filberts with 1 teaspoon vanilla extract

Unmold the chilled custard into the pastry shell. Arrange the cooled rhubarb slices in a sunburst pattern over the custard.

GLAZE

¾ cup reserved syrup from
   the cooked rhubarb,
   strained
¾ cup currant jelly
¼ cup sugar

For how to prepare the glaze, see *Bayerischer Apfelkuchen*. Pour hot glaze over the rhubarb.

    Refrigerate the tart and serve within a few hours.
    Serving Suggestion. Serve with *Schlagsahne* (whipped cream).

Obsttörtchen (fruit tartlets)

    These little pastry shells may be baked several days before they are filled. Use any of the fillings suitable for tarts using a fully baked shell, or try one of the ideas suggested below. Either way, tartlets make a wonderful tasting and very pretty dessert. This recipe makes 10 to 12 tartlets.

Preheat oven to 400°F.
12 round, fluted tart tins
   3½ inches top, 2¼ inches
   bottom, 1⅛ inches deep
Basic rich tart pastry,
   pages 31-37.

If you do not have this size, use others. The recipe may, however, give more or fewer tartlets accordingly.
Use any of the recipes.

    Follow the instructions for how to make rich tart pastry. On wax paper, roll out the dough to a little less than ⅛ inch thick. Place the tins upside down over the dough about ½ inch apart. Press them very lightly into the dough, just enough to make a visible mark. Take the tart tins off and add about ¼ inch to the circle. Cut out with a knife or pastry wheel. Pick up the cut-out dough with an icing spatula or wide-bladed knife and transfer to the mold, which need not be buttered or floured. Shape with your fingers to fit the tin. Knead together the leftover dough, refrigerate until firm again, and roll out to shape the rest of the pastry.
    Prick the bottom of the dough several times with a fork. Place into each mold a piece of buttered aluminum foil or baking parchment filled with beans to weight down the bottom and keep the sides from collapsing.
    Place the molds on a baking sheet and bake in the middle of a preheated 400°F oven for about 8 minutes, or until the pastry looks set and the sides change color slightly. Take out of the oven and remove beans and foil. Again prick the bottom of dough. Place back into oven and bake for another 5 to 8 minutes, or until the pastry shrinks from sides and has a golden color.
    Let the shells cool to warm and then unmold onto a wire rack.

Vanilla cream, page 154.	Fill half of each shell with custard.
Any fruit: fresh, frozen, or canned	Place well-drained fruit decoratively on top of the custard.
Choose one of the glazes, page 167.	Glaze the fruit. If you wish, decorate with leftover cream or whipped cream.

The tartlets are at their best when served soon after filling.

Variations. Instead of vanilla cream, whip up one-half pint of whipping cream. Or try 1 pint of whipped cream with some puréed fruit. Fill the shell completely and decorate with fruit.

Franchipantörtchen (frangipane tartlets)

In the first-class coffeehouses of Germany one can usually order this delicious almond-filled *Törtchen*. The filling is quite easy to make and it freezes very well, if you want to make it ahead of time. This recipe makes 10 to 12 tartlets.

Basic rich tart pastry, pages 31-37.	Use any of the recipes. See the previous recipe, fruit tartlets, for mold size and instructions for lining the mold.

Preheat oven to 400°F.

FILLING

1 cup (2 sticks) unsalted butter, softened 1 cup sugar 4 eggs, at room temperature ½ teaspoon almond extract grated peel of 1 lemon 2½ cups finely ground, blanched almonds 1½ tablespoons flour	With a wire whip or electric mixer, beat butter until creamy and fluffy. Add the sugar and eggs, one at a time. When well blended, add flavoring, almonds, and flour.

Place about 2 tablespoons of filling into each dough-lined mold. Set molds on a baking sheet and bake in the middle of a preheated 400°F oven for about 25 minutes, or until the filling is light brown and the pastry shrinks from the sides and is golden in color. In case the filling browns prematurely, place a piece of aluminum foil on top of tarts.

Let cool until they are warm, and unmold onto a wire rack.

Variations: Franchipantörtchen are often made with a bit of apricot preserves embedded in them. If you would like to try this, place 1 teaspoon of preserves into the dough-lined mold before adding the filling.

Biskuit
(spongecake)

How can one word have come to mean so many different things? In America, biscuits were originally unleavened, dry, flat cakes. Nowadays, of course, they are raised with baking powder or soda, and almost always served hot. For the English, biscuit (or the earlier form "bisket" which is still pronounced as such) is what Americans call a cookie or cracker. For the Germans, it has a different meaning altogether. The modern German *Biskuit* is a cake whose batter is made without the addition of butter, in America called a spongecake. Finally, just to make things a bit more complicated, there exists a buttered cousin of this spongecake, known as *Butterbiskuit* or *Genueser Biskuit*, which is described in the second part of this section.

Biskuit is the classical batter for *Torten* (layer cakes), "tortelettes," jelly and cream rolls, ladyfingers, and various cookies. Since this cake is itself so very light, one can splurge with rich fillings of buttercream or whipped cream, with frostings and glazes. With spongecake as the base, your imagination is the only limit in creating variations for your own house specialty torte. But who could resist a perfectly baked spongecake with just a light dusting of powdered sugar?

Well wrapped, *Biskuit* can be depended upon to keep in the freezer for several months. It is often nice to have such a basic cake in storage and on hand for further improvisation.

Preparing the Pan

Biskuit is traditionally baked in a springform pan. If the cake is made into a torte, it is cut through one or two times for the filling. Individual layer pans may be used if no springform pan is available.

The whole pan should be buttered and floured *and* lined on the bottom only with lightweight aluminum foil or baking parchment. Place the pan on top of the foil, trace the shape, and cut out with scissors. It is then easy to fit the precut foil to the pan bottom. Lightly butter the cake side of the foil before placing it into the pan.

In case of a *Biskuit Rolle* (jelly or cream roll), line the bottom and sides of a baking sheet with foil or baking parchment; butter the bottom lightly.

The pan should not be more than three-fourths full, as the cake needs room to expand.

Preparing the Batter

Eggs are the heart and soul of a spongecake batter, and whether you succeed with your cake depends entirely on how much air you beat into them. Have all your utensils and ingredients ready, since you will not want to stop after starting the batter. Eggs should be at room temperature: chilled egg whites do not fluff satisfactorily. Sift flour: cake flour is preferable since with less gluten it absorbs less moisture than the all-purpose variety.

Here are three different methods for arriving at a perfectly beaten *Biskuit*.

Method I.

This method, known as *Blitzbiskuit* (lightning spongecake), is the most commonly used in modern Germany. You must lavish care in the beating of the egg whites. Sugar is then added when the whites are forming soft peaks and the mixture is further beaten until very stiff. The egg yolks are only folded in gently. This batter has more "body," which is preferable for layer cakes and particularly helpful when melted butter (for butter spongecake) or a small amount of nuts is added. The texture of this cake is very light but at the same time a bit firmer than batters made with Method II.

By Hand. Utensils must be clean and absolutely fat free, otherwise the egg whites will not mount properly. (If the beating of egg whites is new to you, please turn to pages 4-5.)

The working method for making this type of spongecake is nearly the same whether you use elbow grease or an electric mixer. Anchor the bowl to the counter or table top with a suction ring, or place it on a folded wet towel so that you will have a free hand to add ingredients. Sit comfortably, place the egg whites in the bowl, and start to beat with a wire whip. For six egg whites it will take about 10 minutes of continuous beating. When the egg whites form soft peaks, add the sugar by spoonfuls, plus the salt. Continue beating until the mixture is very thick. Add lemon juice to stabilize the egg whites, together with grated lemon peel or other flavorings. Beat a few minutes longer, or until the mixture is thick enough to cling to the whip in a large glob. Finally, add the egg yolks, one by one, stirring just enough to blend.

Fold in one-fourth of the flour, using the whip. Very gently stir in the rest of the flour, going down to the bottom of the bowl and up along the sides, until all of the flour (or nuts or cocoa) is incorporated. It is important to do this as easily and gently as possible in order not to deflate the tiny bubbles of egg white.

Immediately pour the batter into the prepared pan. Gently tilt the pan to start the batter clinging to the sides, and place directly into the preheated oven.

With Electric Mixer. The procedure is essentially the same as with the hand method: read the above first.

The important thing to remember is to use the lowest setting of the mixer for beating the egg whites until they are foamy. Slowly increase speed and beat until they form soft peaks. Add sugar by spoonfuls, plus a pinch of salt, and beat the mixture until thick. Add lemon juice, grated lemon peel or other flavorings, and continue beating; the mixture should be thick enough to cling to the beater in a large glob. Turn mixer to the lowest setting and add the yolks one at a time, just barely blending them.

At this point, revert to a wire whip for folding in the flour, as described in the hand method. An electric mixer is unsatisfactory for this procedure, which must be done very gently.

Method II

In this classic method, eggs and sugar are beaten by hand in a hot water bath; or you may dispense with the water bath and simply use an electric mixer to more easily accomplish almost the same thing. Spongecakes made either way will be soft to the touch and therefore perfect for a spongecake roll which needs to be rolled up without breaking.

With Electric Mixer. Break whole eggs into a mixing bowl and start beating on medium until they are foamy. Add sugar by spoonfuls, salt, and flavoring. Increase speed to medium high and beat the mixture until it is very thick and pale yellow in color. At this point, change to a wire whip for folding in the flour. (A wire whip works better than a spatula, since it is necessary that the incorporation of flour be as complete as possible.) Sift one-half of the flour into the egg mixture. Very gently stir it under the mixture, going down to the bottom of the bowl and up along the sides. Add the other half, working as quickly and gently as you can in order not to deflate the batter.

Pour the batter onto the prepared baking sheet at once and bake as directed by the recipe.

By Hand. Prepare ingredients and utensils as above. Break eggs into a bowl, set over hot, not quite simmering, water. Keep flame at its lowest. Start beating, slowly adding sugar, salt, and flavoring. When mixture begins to fluff up and thicken, remove the bowl from the water, but continue beating until it is very thick and pale yellow in color.

Fold in the flour very gently, as above.

Method III

Good results are obtained by this method in which flour is largely or completely replaced by nuts (or nuts and chocolate). Egg yolks and sugar are beaten together until light and fluffy. The whites are then beaten separately until stiff and folded in alternately with the nuts. A few recipes for tortes will ask for this method.

By Hand and by Mixer. Divide the eggs. Beat egg yolks and sugar with a wire whip or electric mixer until the sugar is dissolved. The mixture will look pale yellow and be light and fluffy.

In a separate bowl, beat egg whites until stiff (see pages 4-5). By hand (do not use an electric mixer for this task, as it will overmix), add half of the flour or nuts and half of the stiffly beaten egg whites to the egg yolk-sugar mixture. With a wire whip fold together very gently. Add remaining flour or nuts and fold again. Finally, add the rest of the whites and fold in rapidly so as not to deflate the batter.

Immediately pour the batter into the prepared pan, tilting the pan to start the batter clinging to the sides, and place directly into the preheated oven.

Making Butter Spongecake

Prepare as in Method I (by mixer or by hand) for spongecake, but add butter after the flour has been folded in.

Melt the unsalted butter in a saucepan before starting with the beating of the eggs. Skim off the residue of milk solids. By the time you are ready to add the butter it should be warm, but no longer hot.

After the flour has been folded into the batter, add one-third of the melted butter and fold it in rapidly but gently with a wire whip. Fold in the rest, being careful not to overmix, since this might deflate the batter.

Bake immediately in a prepared pan so that the butter will not settle to the bottom.

In the Oven

A spongecake batter should be baked immediately, at a slow and even oven temperature, not exceeding 350°F. Place the pan gently at the center of the rack and keep the oven door closed for at least 20 minutes; otherwise the cake may deflate. Avoid overbaking, as this will produce a crumbly, dried-out cake which will break if you attempt to use it for a spongecake roll. Of course, underbaking is equally bad, as doughy spots will make the cake collapse when it is cooling. So keep a close watch on the cake around the time indicated in the recipe when it ought to be done.

Unmolding a **Biskuit**

The cake is done when a cake tester inserted in the middle comes out clean and the top springs back when pressed gently. If you baked the spongecake in a springform or layer pan lined with foil or baking parchment, follow this procedure: let the cake rest for five minutes so moisture can escape and the cake can settle a bit. Take a sharp knife and make a clean cut all the way around the sides of the pan to loosen the cake. If you are using a springform pan, unbuckle it. Line a cake rack with buttered and floured foil or wax paper (otherwise the top of the cake will stick on to the rack). Place the rack on top of the cake and invert the cake with the rack. Remove the pan and immediately peel off the exposed foil or parchment on the bottom of the cake. You may now either turn the cake right-side-up on another rack, or let it cool in the inverted position. If the cake is better shaped—flatter, with squarer sides—on the bottom, you can leave it inverted and serve it that way.

Cool the cake thoroughly before serving, or let the cake rest overnight if you plan to cut it through for one or more layers.

Unmolding a *Biskuitrolle* (Jelly Roll)

Filling with Preserves. After testing to see if the cake is baked, reverse the baking sheet immediately onto a flat surface and peel off the foil or paper. Spread a thin layer of preserves on it. Roll it up, trying not to crack the cake. Place on a serving platter with the seam on the bottom. When the jelly roll has cooled, dust with confectioners sugar.

Filling with Custard, Butter, or Whipped Cream. Since these fillings cannot be placed into a hot cake, the cake must be rolled when hot, then cooled, and finally unrolled and filled.

Place a large clean linen towel (not terry cloth) on a flat surface. Unmold the cake onto the towel and peel off the foil or paper. Carefully roll up the cake and the towel together, and cool with the seam on the bottom. When the cake is cold, gently unroll it. It is impossible to flatten it completely without cracking it, but you will be able to open it enough to spread in the filling.

Note: It is easy to freeze the cake and towel together to fill and serve it at a later time.

Some Serving Ideas

Give your spongecake a light dusting of confectioners sugar or use a frosting of your choice. If the cake is turned into a torte, proceed with the directions given on pages 75-77 on *Torten*.

A three (or two) layer torte can easily consist of different kinds of spongecake. For instance, chocolate, filbert, and basic spongecake can be combined with your choice of buttercream, whipped cream, custard, preserves, or fresh fruit purée. Decorations are always pleasing to the eye; fill a pastry bag with butter or whipped cream and try your hand at it. Chocolates, *Krokant*, and marzipan can be used for special accents.

Disaster Contingency Plan. Finally, have no fear if things go wrong and your spongecake fails to rise. No matter what the result, your cake can be left to dry out completely for a few days. It may then be very finely crumbled and used for crumbs in various *Torten* (see section on *Torten*).

Biskuit (basic spongecake)

Of all the spongecake recipes I have encountered, I find this is one of the best balanced.

Nut and chocolate spongecakes are simply variations on this theme, though I will give their recipes separately.

Preheat oven to 350°F.
9-inch springform pan — Butter and flour the pan. Line the bottom of the pan with foil and butter lightly.

BATTER

6 egg whites — Use Method I, pages 64-65, for preparing the batter.

¾ cup sugar
pinch of salt
1 tablespoon lemon juice
grated peel of ½ lemon
6 egg yolks
1¼ cups sifted cake flour

Pour the batter immediately into the prepared pan and bake on the lowest rack of a preheated 350°F oven for 30 to 35 minutes, or until a cake tester inserted in the middle comes out clean. Let cool in the pan for 5 minutes and unmold as described on page 66.

Haselnussbiskuit (filbert spongecake)

The filberts naturally impart their own flavor to this cake, but they also give it added moisture. A chocolate frosting goes excellently with it.

Preheat oven to 350°F.
9-inch springform pan — Butter and flour the pan. Line the bottom of the pan with foil and butter lightly.

BATTER

6 egg whites — Use Method I, pages 64-65, for preparing the batter.
¾ cup sugar
pinch of salt
1 tablespoon lemon juice
grated peel of ½ lemon
6 egg yolks
1 cup sifted cake flour
½ cup finely ground filberts

Pour the batter immediately into the prepared pan and bake on the lowest rack of a preheated 350°F oven for 30 to 35 minutes, or until a cake tester inserted in the middle comes out clean. Let cool in the pan for 5 minutes and unmold as described on page 66.

Mandelbiskuit (almond spongecake)

One must be discriminating in the choice of flavors to go with this cake because the fragile flavor of the almonds is easily lost. I have found that the old standbys, vanilla and chocolate, do best with it. You may want to decorate it with sliced almonds.

Preheat oven to 350°F.
9-inch springform pan   Butter and flour the pan. Line the bottom of the pan with foil and butter lightly.

BATTER

6 egg whites
¾ cup sugar
pinch of salt
1 tablespoon lemon juice
¼ teaspoon almond extract
6 egg yolks
1 cup sifted cake flour
½ cup finely ground, blanched almonds

Use Method I, pages 64-65, for preparing the batter.

Pour the batter immediately into the prepared pan and bake on the lowest rack of a preheated 350°F oven for 30 to 35 minutes, or until a cake tester inserted in the middle comes out clean. Let cool in the pan for 5 minutes and unmold as described on page 66.

Schokoladenbiskuit (chocolate spongecake)

A rum-flavored frosting or a vanilla or mocha filling are perfect accompaniments for this standard favorite.

Preheat oven to 350°F.
9-inch springform pan   Butter and flour the pan. Line the bottom of the pan with foil and butter lightly.

BATTER

6 egg whites
¾ cup sugar
pinch of salt
1 tablespoon lemon juice
grated peel of ½ lemon
6 egg yolks
1 cup sifted cake flour
⅓ cup sifted cocoa

Use Method I, pages 64-65, for preparing the batter.

Immediately pour the batter into the prepared pan and bake on the lowest rack of a preheated 350°F oven for 30 to 35 minutes, or until a cake tester inserted in the middle comes out clean. Let cool in the pan for 5 minutes and unmold as described on page 66.

Biskuitrolle (jelly roll)

A rolled spongecake is simple to make, and yet the beautiful spiral pattern always looks impressive. You can bake and fill a cake roll in just an hour's time; it is often useful to have such a recipe in your repertoire.

It takes one cup of preserves to fill the inside of this roll. Use another cup to cover the outside, or dust the cake with confectioners sugar. If the preserves are too thick to spread easily, heat them a bit or mix in one or two tablespoons rum or cognac (orange liqueur if you are using orange marmalade).

Preheat oven to 375°F.

16 x 11 x 1-inch jelly-roll pan	Line the sheet with foil or baking parchment and butter the bottom lightly.

BATTER

4 eggs	Use Method II, page 65, for preparing the batter.
⅓ cup sugar	
1 teaspoon vanilla extract	
Or	
grated peel of ½ lemon	
⅔ cup sifted cake flour	

Pour the batter immediately into the prepared baking sheet and bake on the middle level of a 375°F oven for 12 to 15 minutes, or until a cake tester inserted comes out clean. Unmold the cake right away, as described on pages 66-67.

Schokolade Biskuitrolle (chocolate spongecake roll)

You may wish to fill this roll with kirsch-flavored whipped cream, folding in some tart cherries. If so, also decorate with cherries.

Preheat oven to 375°F.

16 x 11 x 1-inch jelly-roll pan	Line the sheet with foil or baking parchment and butter the bottom lightly.

BATTER

4 eggs	Use Method II, page 65, for preparing the batter.
½ cup sugar	
1 teaspoon vanilla extract	
½ cup sifted cake flour	
¼ cup sifted cocoa	

Pour the batter immediately into the prepared baking sheet and bake on the middle level of a 375°F oven for 12 to 15 minutes, or until a cake tester inserted comes out clean. Unmold the cake right away, as described on pages 66-67.

Biskuitrolle mit schlagsahne
(spongecake roll with whipped cream)

This recipe is my mother's, and I have wonderful memories of the first strawberries from our garden being used in it. It is a refreshing treat and a perfect dessert.

Use the master recipe for a jelly roll, page 70.

Let the cake, rolled in a towel, cool completely.

FILLING

2 cups strawberries, blueberries, raspberries, or any other fruit you may like, fresh, frozen, or canned

Chop strawberries or peaches into little chunks. Drain the fruit well. Leave small berries whole. Set aside some fruit for decoration.

1 pint (2 cups) whipping cream
4 tablespoons confectioners sugar
1½ tablespoons rum
   Or
¼ teaspoon almond extract if blueberries are used

Whip cream until stiff. Add the flavoring.

Unwrap the cooled cake, being careful not to break it. Fold into the chopped fruit about 2 cups of whipped cream and spread this mixture inside the roll using a spatula or wide knife. Gently roll up the cake and transfer to a serving platter, placing the seam on the bottom. Cover the cake with the remaining whipped cream, leaving some aside for decoration if you wish. With the tines of a fork, comb a series of furrows in the cream lengthwise down the roll. Make whipped cream rosettes with a pastry bag and decorate with fruit.

Refrigerate until serving.

Baumstamm (chocolate log)

Furrowed chocolate cream gives an authentic looking bark to this little "tree trunk." A delight to see and to eat.

Use the master recipe for a jelly roll, page 70.
Chocolate buttercream with custard base, pages 153-154.

Let the cake, rolled in a towel, cool completely.

Open the cake roll gently and spread about 1 cup of chocolate cream into it. Roll up again and place on a serving platter, seam down. Spread one-half cup of cream over the outside of the roll. Fill the remaining cream into a pastry bag with a ribbon tube opening and improvise a bark surface on the roll. Give it a rough textured look with little circles to indicate knots. As a final touch, sprinkle very lightly with medium-ground chocolate.

Refrigerate until serving or freeze.

Butter Biskuit (butter spongecake)

This wonderful cake, which the Germans call *Genueser Biskuit, Butter Biskuit* or *Blitzkuchen* and the French call *Genoise,* comes from Italy. It combines the feathery lightness of a spongecake with the moistness and keeping qualities of cakes belonging to the *Rührkuchen* family.

Butter spongecake is used as the base for *Torten* or for petits fours, or it is simply enjoyed plain. As with its butterless cousin, you can set your imagination to work, choosing a frosting or filling to suit your fancy.

Preheat oven to 350°F.

9-inch springform pan	Butter and flour the pan. Line the bottom of the pan with foil and butter lightly.

BATTER

6 egg whites	See page 66 for preparing the batter.

1 cup sugar
pinch of salt
1 tablespoon lemon juice
grated peel of ½ lemon
6 egg yolks
1½ cups sifted cake flour
½ cup (1 stick) unsalted
    butter, melted

Pour immediately into the prepared pan and bake on the lowest rack of a preheated 350°F oven for 40 minutes, or until a cake tester inserted in the middle comes out clean. Let cool in the pan for 5 minutes and unmold as described on page 66.

Nuss Butter Biskuit (nut butter spongecake)

Use your choice of either filberts, almonds, or walnuts for this fine cake.

Preheat oven to 350°F.

9-inch springform pan	Butter and flour the pan. Line the bottom of the pan with foil and butter lightly.

	BATTER
6 egg whites	See page 66 for preparing the batter.

1 cup sugar
pinch of salt
1 tablespoon lemon juice
grated peel of ½ lemon
6 egg yolks
1¼ cups sifted cake flour
½ cup finely ground filberts, almonds, or walnuts
½ cup (1 stick) unsalted butter, melted

    Pour immediately into the prepared pan and bake on the lowest rack of a preheated 350°F oven for 40 minutes, or until a cake tester inserted in the middle comes out clean. Let cool in the pan for 5 minutes and unmold as described on page 66.

Schokoladen Butter Biskuit (chocolate butter spongecake)

    Fill this cake with rum- or almond-flavored whipped cream or a layer of nut buttercream.

Preheat oven to 350°F.

9-inch springform pan	Butter and flour the pan. Line the bottom of the pan with foil and butter lightly.
	BATTER
6 egg whites	See page 66 for preparing the batter.

1 cup sugar
pinch of salt
1 tablespoon lemon juice
grated peel of ½ lemon
6 egg yolks
1¼ cups sifted cake flour
⅓ cup sifted cocoa
½ cup (1 stick) unsalted butter, melted

    Pour immediately into the prepared pan and bake on the lowest rack of a preheated 350°F oven for 40 minutes, or until a cake tester inserted in the middle comes out clean. Let cool in the pan for 5 minutes and unmold as described on page 66.

Orangen Butter Biskuit (orange butter spongecake)

I like to serve this cake with a coating of orange-flavored fondant decorated with orange slices.

Preheat oven to 350°F.

9-inch springform pan | Butter and flour the pan. Line the bottom of the pan with foil and butter lightly.

BATTER

6 egg whites | See page 66 for preparing the batter.

1 cup sugar
pinch of salt
1 tablespoon frozen, concen-
    trated orange juice,
    thawed
grated peel of 1 orange
6 egg yolks
1½ cups sifted cake flour
½ cup (1 stick) unsalted
    butter, melted

Pour immediately into the prepared pan and bake on the lowest rack of a preheated 350°F oven for 40 minutes, or until a cake tester inserted in the middle comes out clean. Let cool in the pan for 5 minutes and unmold as described on page 66.

Torten

(tortes)

These delicate cakes, rich with fillings, frostings, and decorations, have a long and sweet history. Early inhabitants of what is now called Germany made flour and honey into thin rounds and served them at Midsummer Festival to symbolize the sun. Out of those round, sweet things developed the filled and artfully decorated "Tarten" of the Middle Ages. These were created in the kitchens of cloisters and castles and enjoyed by the wealthy classes. Our modern tortes have changed considerably in taste from those served a few hundred years ago, but they still have several things in common. Like its ancestors, the modern torte is a very special treat, served on festive occasions; in Germany tortes are considered *Fest Gebäck* (festive cakes). With tortes, one does not spare eggs, butter, liqueurs, nuts, and other fine ingredients, nor does one save on the time required to create these handcrafted specialties.

Luckily, however, tortes can be made at leisure and frozen to wait for a special occasion. If you decide on a fresh fruit topping with a glaze, it is better to add this the same day you serve the torte; still, it can be baked and otherwise filled ahead of time.

Filling a Torte

For successful frosting and decorating, one must start with a well-shaped cake. If the cake is defective in this respect, there is nothing wrong with resorting to a little surgery. A dome-shaped cake may have its top sliced off, and may be turned upside down. A sunken middle can be corrected by placing more filling toward the center of the cake.

To successfully cut the cake horizontally, a long sharp knife, or a thread, along with a good eye are needed. If you are using a knife, insert it from the side to the center of the cake and slowly turn the cake, trying to keep the knife as level as possible, until it is completely cut. Another method involves encompassing the circumference of the cake with a strong thread. Pull the thread slowly together until the layer is separated. With either procedure the result may not be exactly straight. This is all right, however, so long as when you place the layers back together after filling, they are lined up precisely in the same position in which they were cut. To make the alignment, insert a toothpick into the side of each layer at the same place on the circumference. After filling the cake, replace the top layer with its toothpick over the toothpick in the bottom layer, and you can expect a perfect fit.

To transport a layer, lift its edge and place a piece of wax paper under it. Work the paper all the way under the layer and lift it by holding the edges of the paper. When the cake is filled, pick up the layer with the paper again, line up the toothpicks, and hold it over the filling. Tilt the top until one edge almost touches the edge of the bottom layer. From there you should be able to slide the paper back gradually as you lower the top layer onto the filling.

Frosting a Torte

Brush away all loose crumbs. Spread a thin layer of hot apricot preserves (page 166) over the cake and let dry for a few minutes. This important step (which German bakers call *apricotieren*) will help to give a smooth surface and seal the cake so the frosting will not be absorbed.

Tortes which receive an overall frosting should be set on a cake rack, so excess frosting can run off freely. However, if a torte is to receive a high filling or is otherwise very fragile, you will not want to move it after it has been filled or frosted. In such a case, place the bottom layer of the cake on the serving platter. Cut out four long, wide strips of paper, place them about 1 inch under the layer (the rest should cover the platter), and proceed with filling and frosting the torte. When the frosting is dry, remove the paper, which will leave you with a clean serving platter.

For filling one layer and frosting a torte, you will need approximately the following amounts:

For an 8-inch cake, 1½ cups
For a 9-inch cake, 2 cups
For a 10-inch cake, 2½ cups
For an additional layer, add about 1 cup

About Decorating

Once the torte is covered with a topping (which may or may not coat the sides), there is no limit to the ways you can decorate it: chocolates, nougat pieces, almond paste, fresh fruit, candied fruit or flowers, rosettes of buttercream or whipped cream, or whatever your imagination can invent. You may be satisfied with a simple design, or you may go in for baroque flourishes. However, some tortes have their own traditional decoration; for instance, a *Schwarzwälder Kirschtorte* (Black Forest Cherry Torte) or a *Frankfurter Kranz* would not be what they are if you did not dress them properly. For most tortes, the classic way to cover the sides is with toasted, sliced nuts (almonds, filberts, walnuts), or shaved or medium-ground chocolate. This can be directly brushed over buttercream or whipped cream. If a torte already has a frosting which has set, cover the sides with apricot preserves and brush on the nuts or chocolate.

A pastry bag, preferably the type lined with plastic, along with a variety of pastry tubes, will help you to make the decorations. The bag should be no more than two-thirds full. The best way to control the decorating process is to twist the unfilled part of the bag so that the filling is pressed out of the tube nozzle. A ribbon tube, a small and large open star tube, and a plain tube should give enough variety of design. For writing on a torte, use the smallest tube available.

About Storage and Freezing

When the torte is filled and decorated, place it in the refrigerator or at a cool spot in your house. Cake platters with a plastic dome come in handy here. If the torte is very cold, let it stand before serving at room temperature for a time so that it can regain its full flavor and aroma.

If a torte is to be stored for more than one or two days, place in the freezer without wrapping. When thoroughly frozen, it can be wrapped and then stored for a few months. A very useful device for this is something called a "cake saver." This is simply a large plastic container for refrigerating and freezing cakes. If you can find one, buy the 12-inch diameter size for 9 to 10-inch tortes.

When a torte has been frozen, be sure to give it enough time to thaw before serving, in order for the flavors to develop. Since cake is a natural "insulating foam," thawing may take two or three hours.

Slicing a Torte

A long, sharp, and *hot* knife does an excellent job in slicing a cake or torte. Hold the knife momentarily under very hot water, dry, and use immediately.

Here are some approximate figures on serving capacities. Much depends, of course, on the thickness (and the richness!) of the torte.

A 10-inch torte yields 16 slices.

A 9-inch torte yields 12 to 16 slices (if you plan to decorate each separate piece, try only for 12 pieces, as 16 may look too crowded).

An 8-inch torte yields 8 to 10 slices.

A spongecake roll made in a 16 x 11 x 1-inch jelly-roll pan yields about 12 slices.

Torten 77

Schwarzwälder Kirschtorte (Black Forest cherry torte)

In the minds of many aficionados the high point of German bakery art is the elegant *Schwarzwälder Kirschtorte.* Its name comes from the cherry brandy (known as *Kirsch*) made in the Black Forest region of Germany. This liqueur lends a unique flavor to the torte. If you can obtain imported kirsch, by all means do so, since American kirsch has a faint flavor of bitter almonds and is not really a perfect substitute.

Use only red sour cherries for this torte, since only they have the needed tart flavor.

Preheat oven to 375°F.
9-inch springform pan or Butter and flour the pan(s).
   3 cake layer pans

BATTER

4½ ounces semisweet chocolate	In a double boiler, melt chocolate over barely simmering water. Set aside to cool.
½ ounce unsweetened chocolate	
½ cup plus 4 tablespoons (1½ sticks) unsalted butter	Cream butter, sugar, and egg yolks, using one of the methods on pages 11-13.
1¼ cups sugar	
6 egg yolks	
2 tablespoons kirsch	Add the kirsch.
1⅔ cups sifted cake flour	With a wire whip, alternately fold in flour, baking powder, and chocolate.
2 teaspoons baking powder	
melted chocolate as above	
6 egg whites	Beat egg whites separately and fold gently into the batter.

Pour the batter at once into the prepared pan and bake on the lower middle of a preheated 375°F oven for 50 to 55 minutes (only about 15 minutes for layer pans), or until a cake tester inserted in the middle comes out clean. Cool in the pan for 10 minutes before unmolding it onto a cake rack to cool thoroughly.

Leave the cake bottom side up to make the torte.

ASSEMBLING THE TORTE

1½ pounds red tart cherries Drain cherries well in a colander. Set aside
   fresh, frozen, or canned   12 to 16 cherries for decoration (depending
   (about 4 cups)   on how many pieces you plan to slice).

Slice the torte in three approximately equal layers (see page 75). Pull foil or wax paper under the layers in order to move them without breaking. When you have prepared the three layers, make the filling.

FILLING

1 pint whipping cream   Whip cream until stiff. Add the kirsch.
6 tablespoons confectioners
   sugar
⅓ cup kirsch

Evenly spread one-half cup of the whipped cream over the bottom layer. Fill 1 cup of cream into a pastry bag and design three large, high rings on top of the cream. Fill these out with cherries. Carefully place the second layer on top of the whipped cream and cherry design. Spread about 1 cup of whipped cream on this second layer, covering it with the top layer. Now there are 1½ cups of whipped cream left. Save one-half cup for the decoration and spread the rest over the top and sides of the torte. Lightly slash markings for 12 or 16 pieces in the whipped cream on top of the torte.

½ cup of whipped cream	On the outside edge of each piece make a rosette with the pastry bag. Fill each rosette with a cherry.
1 ounce shaved, semisweet chocolate, page 173.	Decorate the top with shaved chocolate, as shown in the color section

Refrigerate the torte until serving.

Käsesahne-Torte (quark cream torte)

If you have tried some of the *Kuchen* and *Torten* which use *Quark* and have grown fond of it, here is an all *Quark* torte for your delectation. The filling is made creamy and light with whipped cream, flavored with lemon juice, and placed between two layers of spongecake.

9-inch basic spongecake (see master recipe, page 68).	Let the cake rest for one day before cutting it into 2 layers.

FILLING

½ pint whipping cream 2 tablespoons confectioners sugar	Whip cream until stiff. Chill until needed.
3 cups *Quark,* pages 149-151 2 egg yolks ½ cup sugar grated peel of ½ lemon ½ teaspoon vanilla extract	Beat *Quark* until smooth. Add egg yolks, Mix in the sugar and flavoring.
1½ envelopes (1½ tablespoons) unflavored, powdered gelatin 3 tablespoons lemon juice 1-2 tablespoons water whipped cream as above	Dissolve gelatin with with lemon juice and water over low heat. Let cool until it is warm (it should not be hot) and beat into the *Quark* mixture. With a spatula, fold the whipped cream into it. Chill until thickened to spreading consistency (about 15 minutes).

In the meantime, slice the cake horizontally into two layers. Move aside the top layer with a piece of foil (see page 75), and cut the pattern for 12 to 16 slices with a thread or knife. Place the bottom layer on a serving platter: once the filling is spread you won't be able to move the torte without breaking. With a spatula, spread the *Quark* cream evenly over the bottom layer. It will be a high filling. Very carefully move the top layer back.

Chill for at least a few hours before serving so the cream can set some more. Before serving, dust the top generously with confectioners sugar.

Frankfurter Kranz (Frankfurt crown)

From its rum-flavored filling to its trimming of crushed almond brittle, the *Frankfurter Kranz* is a marvel. Bake it a day ahead of time and fill it several hours before serving, so that the flavors can blend.

Preheat oven to 375°F.

9-inch tube pan or *Gugelhopf* mold, holding 2½ to 3 quarts. Note: The traditional pan for this torte is a *Kranzform*, a kind of unfluted *Gugelhopf* mold unavailable in the U.S. Virtually any tube pan is acceptable as a substitute.	Butter and flour the pan.

BATTER

1 cup plus 2 tablespoons unsalted butter 1⅓ cups sugar 6 egg yolks	Cream butter, sugar and egg yolks, using one of the methods on pages 11-13.
1½ teaspoons vanilla extract 1½ tablespoons dark rum grated peel of ½ lemon	Add vanilla, rum, and lemon peel.
2½ cups sifted flour 2 teaspoons baking powder	Fold in flour and baking powder.
6 egg whites	Beat egg whites separately and fold gently into the batter.

Pour at once into the prepared pan and bake on the lowest rack of a preheated 375°F oven for 50 to 60 minutes, or until a cake tester inserted in the center comes out clean. Cool in the pan for 10 minutes before unmolding it onto a cake rack to cool thoroughly.

Filling and Frosting the Torte. The *Frankfurter Kranz* can be filled and frosted either with whipped cream or buttercream.

SCHLAGSAHNE (WHIPPED CREAM)

1 pint (2 cups) whipping cream 4 tablespoons confectioners sugar 2½ tablespoons dark rum	Whip cream until stiff. Add the rum.

80 Torten

Buttercream, page 152, flavored
    with rum; increase recipe
    by one-half

    Slice the cake through twice (or three times) with a long, sharp knife to form three (or four) layers. Carefully set them aside.

    Reserve about 2 cups of filling, 1⅔ cups for frosting and ⅓ cup for decoration. Spread each layer with an equal amount of the remaining cream.

    When the torte is filled, frost the outside smoothly, using an icing spatula or a broad-bladed knife. Frost the inside ring also.

Krokant (toasted almond brittle) master recipe, page 170	Brush or drop the *Krokant* on the torte until the frosting is completely and evenly covered.
reserved buttercream or whipped cream	Fill a pastry bag with the cream. Using a star tube, make about 8 rosettes on top of the torte.
8 maraschino cherries	Fill each rosette with a cherry.

Haselnusstorte (filbert torte)

    One of my sister Gertrud's specialties. Her torte is covered with chocolate sugar frosting and decorated with either whole filberts or almonds. A dollop of whipped cream is, of course, a must!

Preheat oven to 350°F.

9-inch springform pan	Butter and flour the pan. Line the bottom of the pan with foil and butter lightly.

BATTER

8 egg yolks 1¼ cups sugar grated peel of 1 lemon ⅓ cup cake flour 3 cups finely ground filberts	Beat egg yolks with the sugar, using Method III, page 65. Add lemon peel.
8 egg whites	In a separate bowl, beat egg whites until stiff. With a wire whip, fold the flour into the egg-sugar mixture. Follow with half of the filberts and half of the egg whites. Add rest of filberts. Gently fold in the remainder of egg whites.

    Immediately pour the batter into the prepared pan and bake in the middle of a preheated 350°F oven for 50 to 55 minutes, or until a cake tester inserted comes out clean.

    Let the cake rest for 5 minutes before umolding it onto a cake rack.

The torte should be allowed to cool completely before applying the frosting.

1 cup apricot preserves, page 166	With a pastry brush, coat the torte with hot preserves. Allow to dry.
Chocolate sugar frosting (master recipe, page 164)	Set the torte on a cake rack. Pour frosting evenly over top and sides. This frosting needs several hours to set.
Whole, blanched filberts Or Whole blanched almonds	Decorate with the nuts before frosting has set. Make a flower pattern, or simply place one nut on each piece with some in the middle.

Serving Suggestion. Serve with whipped cream, either vanilla flavored or with the addition of filberts.

Schokoladentorte (chocolate torte)

Use one of the Parisian Creams for the filling and frosting for this torte. Either of them will be delicious.

9-inch Chocolate Butter Spongecake	Let the cake rest for one day before cutting it into 2 layers.
Parisian cream, page 156	Move bottom layer of cake onto a serving platter. Allow cream to thicken to spreading consistency. Reserve about 1 cup of cream for frosting and about ½ cup for decoration. Fill the layers with the remaining cream.
1 cup apricot preserves, page 166	Brush entire torte with hot preserves.

Spread top and sides with cream. Mark 12 to 16 pieces on top of torte to serve as a guide when decorating. Fill pastry bag with cream and using a medium star tube make a borderline around the outside edge. Place a rosette on each piece and place one in the center if you wish.

½ cup lightly toasted, medium-ground filberts Or 1 cup *Krokant* (toasted almond brittle), page 170	Brush over the chocolate cream at the sides of torte.

Sahnetorte (whipped cream torte)

This torte is best when filled with freshly beaten whipped cream and served immediately. In case it needs to wait for several hours, add gelatin to the cream; it will keep very well that way.

9-inch basic spongecake (see master recipe, page 68)
About 1 pound of fruit of your choice: strawberries, raspberries, grapes, currants, blueberries, sliced bananas, or fresh or canned peaches or apricots

Allow the cake to rest for one day before cutting it into three layers.
Prepare the fruit and drain in a colander.

FILLING

Optional:
2 teaspoons powdered, unflavored gelatin
1 tablespoon water
1 pint whipping cream
4 tablespoons confectioners sugar
2 teaspoons vanilla extract
Or
1-2 tablespoons rum, kirsch, cognac, or other liqueur, depending on what goes best with the fruit

In a measuring cup, dissolve gelatin with water. Let cool until it is warm; do not allow to gel.
Whip cream (and add gelatin, if used) until stiff. Add flavoring.

Move bottom layer onto a serving platter. Spread about 1 cup of whipped cream on both layers. Move back top layer and cover top and sides with the remaining cream, leaving some aside for decoration. Distribute the fruit in rounds or in a sunburst pattern.

Gelatin glaze, page 167

Spoon the thickened gelatin over the fruit. Refrigerate for a while until gelatin has set.

½ cup sliced, plain almonds
reserved whipped cream

Brush almonds on the sides of torte.
Fill a pastry bag and decorate to your liking.

Mandel-Orangen-Torte (almond orange torte)

Frost the top and sides with orange-flavored fondant. Or leave it plain with a light dusting of confectioners sugar and serve with a dollop of orange-flavored whipped cream.

Preheat oven to 375°F.
10-inch springform pan

Butter and flour the pan. Line the bottom of the pan with foil and butter lightly.

Have a 4½ quart bowl available for beating the batter.

Torten 83

BATTER

7 egg whites 1¼ cups sugar pinch of salt 7 egg yolks	Beat egg whites. Add sugar and yolks, using Method 1, page 64.
1 tablespoon orange liqueur 2 tablespoons frozen, concentrated orange juice, thawed grated peel of ½ orange	Add liqueur, orange juice, and orange rind.
½ cup sifted flour 3 cups finely ground, blanched almonds 1¼ cups spongecake crumbs	With a wire whip first fold in the flour, then add the almonds and crumbs.

Pour immediately into the prepared pan and bake on the lowest rack of a preheated 375°F oven for 35 minutes, or until a cake tester inserted in the middle comes out clean. Cool in the pan for 5 minutes and unmold as described on page 66.

The cake will be at its best if you give it a chance to rest for one day.

1 cup apricot preserves, page 166	Brush the entire torte with hot preserves.
Fondant (master recipe pages 161-163) flavored with: 1 tablespoon concentrated, frozen orange juice, thawed 1-2 tablespoons orange juice, strained	Set the torte on a cake rack and pour fondant over it. Let fondant dry completely, then move it carefully on a serving platter.

If you wish you may decorate the sides of the torte.

Several spoons of apricot preserves	Spread over fondant.
½ cup sliced, lightly toasted almonds	Brush onto preserves.

Frucht-Kuppeltorte (domed fruit torte)

Sweet fruit and tangy *Quark* make such a perfect couple! In this concoction, the filling is built into a grand mound at the center of the torte: a diverting dessert for a summer's afternoon.

9-inch basic spongecake (see master recipe, page 68)	Let the cake rest for a day before cutting it into 2 layers.

FILLING

1 quart strawberries	Wash and hull strawberries. Slice them in halves. Purée 1½ cups in a blender, leaving

	the others to be set on the bottom layer. Set purée and strawberry halves aside until needed.
½ pint whipping cream 2 tablespoons confectioners sugar	Whip cream until stiff. Chill until needed.
3 cups *Quark,* pages 149-151 2 egg yolks ½ cup sugar	Beat *Quark* until smooth. Add egg yolks and sugar. Mix in fruit purée.
2 envelopes (2 tablespoons) unflavored powdered gelatin 3-4 tablespoons dark rum	In a separate saucepan or measuring cup, heat gelatin and rum over medium heat until dissolved (do not boil). Let cool until it is warm and beat into the *Quark*–fruit mixture.
whipped cream as above	With a spatula, fold the whipped cream into it. Chill until fairly thick, otherwise you won't be able to shape it. (It will need about 1 hour to thicken.)

Assembling the Torte. Slice a top layer off the cake, making it as thin as possible without its breaking (about ½ inch). Set the layer aside (transporting it with a piece of wax paper) and cut on it a pattern of 12 to 16 pieces with a knife. Place the bottom layer on a serving platter, as once the torte is filled it will be difficult to move without breaking.

Spread a thin layer of fruit cream on the bottom layer and place strawberries on this. Cover the sides of the torte with cream. Then cover the berries, building up the center, finally making a dome. Very carefully replace the top layer, molding it to the domed filling. Press it down lightly.

½ cup sliced, lightly toasted almonds	Brush almond slices on the side of the torte.

Dust the top generously with confectioners sugar. Chill for at least several hours so the cream can set some more.

Variations. For fruit, try blueberries, raspberries, or freshly sliced peaches.

Orangentorte (orange torte)

The buttercream used for this torte is altogether excellent. Little bite-sized orange balls decorate each piece.

9-inch almond spongecake (see master recipe, page 69) Orange buttercream (master recipe, page 155)	Allow the cake to rest for one day before cutting it into 2 layers. Spread ¾ to 1 cup of buttercream on the first layer. Cover with top layer. Frost the top and sides of torte with the rest of the cream, saving some for decoration, if you wish.

Torten 85

Mark 12 to 16 pieces on top of the torte to serve as a guide when decorating and cutting. Fill the pastry bag and make a continuous ribbon at the outside edge.

12 to 16 orange balls, page 168	Place one on each piece (and perhaps a large one at the center).
½ cup plain, sliced almonds Or 1 cup pulverized nougat	Brush on the side of the torte.

Refrigerate the torte until serving.

Mokkatorte (mocha torte)

Decorated with chocolate truffles or nougat balls (page 169), this torte can be made to look very elegant indeed.

9-inch chocolate spongecake or chocolate butter spongecake	Let the cake rest for one day before cutting it into 2 layers.
Mocha buttercream, pages 151-152	Move bottom layer of cake onto a serving platter. Spread on ¾ cup of buttercream. Carefully move back top layer.
1 cup apricot preserves, p. 166	Brush entire torte with hot preserves.

Spread on top and sides the rest of the cream, leaving some aside for decoration. Mark 12 to 16 pieces on top of the torte to serve as a guide when decorating and cutting. Fill a pastry bag with the remaining cream and make a border around the outside edge, either as one continuous ribbon or as rosettes very close to each other. Decorate each piece with your chosen chocolates.

1 cup nougat or chocolate, ground medium-fine	Brush over the cream at the sides of torte.

Chill the torte before serving.

Karottentorte (carrot torte)

Can carrots make a cake so remarkable that it qualifies for the honored title, *Torte*? When I first tried this recipe, I knew that answer was yes! Many different flavors are united here to perfection and the whole is covered with a fondant frosting. Lovely little marzipan carrots decorate the top.

Preheat oven to 375°F.

9-inch springform pan	Butter and flour the pan. Line the bottom of the pan with foil and butter lightly.

BATTER

7 egg yolks 1 cup sugar	Beat egg yolks with the sugar, using Method III, page 65.

Schwarzwälder Kirschtorte (Black Forest Cherry Torte)

Aprikosenrädchen (Apricot Windmills) and *Nusskämme* (Nut Combs)

2 tablespoons kirsch (imported if possible) pinch of cinnamon pinch of ground cloves grated peel of ½ lemon	Add kirsch and flavorings.
½ cup sifted flour 1½ teaspoons baking powder 1¼ cups finely ground, blanched almonds 1⅔ cups finely ground filberts 1⅓ cups spongecake crumbs 1⅓ cups finely grated, juicy carrots	Mix in flour, baking powder, and half of the nuts.
7 egg whites	In a separate bowl, beat egg whites until stiff. With a wire whip, fold half of the egg whites into the batter. Follow with the rest of the nuts, crumbs, and carrots. Finally, gently fold in the remainder of egg whites.

Pour immediately into the prepared pan and bake on the lowest rack of a preheated 375°F oven for 40 minutes, or until a cake tester inserted in the middle comes out clean. Let cool in the pan for 5 minutes and unmold as described on page 66.

Whether you serve the torte plain, or with the fondant frosting and almond paste, let it rest for at least one day (preferably two) so the flavors can mingle. It will then be at its very best.

For marzipan (almond paste) see master recipe, page 171. (This will be slightly more than you need.) A few drops of red and yellow food coloring	If you wish, knead the color into the almond paste to give the carrots a realistic shading. Form a roll with the marzipan, ¾ to 1 inch in diameter. Cut 12 slices, also between ¾ and 1 inch long. Form out of each slice a little carrot. With a knife make little cuts around them in imitation of those flutings seen on real carrots.
12 pistachios	Choose nice, big nuts and shell them. Blanch for 1 minute in boiling water. Drain and remove the skin. Cut each nut in half; most will fall into halves naturally. Stick two pieces of nut in the carrot to suggest the green stalk. Set aside until needed.
Fondant frosting (master recipe, pages 161-163). Flavor with 2 tablespoons kirsch	Move the torte to a cake rack. Pour on the fondant, either allowing it to run over the sides or spreading it only on the top, as shown in the color section.

Score 12 pieces with a knife on top of the soft fondant. Put the carrots in place, one on each piece (stem at the outer edge of the cake, point toward the center), while the fondant is still soft. It hardens quickly; you will have to work fast.

Several spoons of strained apricot preserves

Spread the preserves on the side of the torte.

½ cup sliced almonds, lightly toasted

Brush nuts over the apricot preserves.

Wiener Schokoladentorte (Viennese chocolate torte)

Spongecake crumbs are substituted for part of the flour in this torte, which also includes finely ground filberts and chocolate. It is cut into two layers, sprinkled with sherry, filled with apricot preserves, and covered with a chocolate frosting. An excellent and very moist affair!

Preheat oven to 350°F.
10-inch springform pan

Butter and flour the pan. Line the bottom of the pan with foil and butter lightly.

Have a 4½ quart bowl available for beating the batter.

BATTER

8 egg whites
⅔ cup sugar
pinch of salt
8 egg yolks

Beat egg whites until they form soft peaks. Add sugar and yolks, using Method I, page 64.

1 tablespoon lemon juice
grated peel of ½ lemon, or
1 teaspoon vanilla extract

Add lemon juice and rind or vanilla.

⅓ cup flour
¾ cup finely grated, semi-sweet chocolate
1½ cups finely ground filberts
1¾ cups spongecake crumbs

With a wire whip first fold in the flour, then add the chocolate, filberts, and crumbs.

Pour immediately into the prepared pan and bake on the lowest rack of a preheated 350°F oven for 35 to 40 minutes, or until a cake tester inserted in the middle comes out clean. (There might be a little chocolate hanging on the tester, so do not mistake it for batter.)

Let cool in the pan for 5 minutes and unmold as described on page 66. The cake should be allowed to rest for one day before filling it.

Assembling the Torte. Slice the cake horizontally into two layers.

⅓ cup cream sherry
⅓ cup apricot preserves

Sprinkle the sherry on top and bottom layer.
Spread a thin layer of preserves on the bottom layer of cake. If it is too thick to be easily spread, heat it in a saucepan until

melted. If you wish, you may rub it through a sieve and leave out the bits of skin.

CHOCOLATE FROSTING

2½ ounces semisweet chocolate	In a double boiler, over barely simmering water, melt chocolate.
½ ounce unsweetened chocolate	
¾ cup confectioners sugar	Add confectioners sugar and egg yolk, stirring it with a wire whip until the mixture is smooth.
1 egg yolk	
4 tablespoons unsalted butter	In a separate saucepan, melt the butter. Turn off heat on double boiler but leave pan in water. Stir the melted butter into the chocolate mixture by droplets.

Pour the frosting over the torte immediately, since it will set very fast. With a wide-bladed knife, improvise a wavy baroque pattern on top. Let the torte set completely (about one hour) before slicing.

Erdbeertorte (strawberry torte)

I adore this recipe, which I owe to my sister, Renate. The spongecake is filled with tasty pastry cream, and the strawberries are glazed with transparent, cool-looking gelatin.

9-inch basic spongecake, (see master recipe, page 68)	Allow the cake to rest for one day before cutting it into two layers.
1 quart strawberries	Wash and hull berries. Drain in a colander; they should be completely dry.
Vanilla cream (master recipe, page 154)	You may leave the vanilla cream plain or fold in whipped cream. If you decide on whipped cream, leave ⅓ cup aside for decoration.

Move the bottom layer of the cake onto a serving platter. Spread on one cup of cream. Cover with top layer and spread rest of cream over top and sides.

Place one big berry in the middle of the torte. Make a round of strawberries on the edge of the torte, the next round close against the first, and so to the center, covering the entire surface.

Chill while making the gelatin.

Gelatin glaze (master recipe, page 167)	Spoon the almost gelled glaze over the fruit. Refrigerate the torte for a while until gelatin has set.
½ cup sliced, plain almonds	Brush almonds on the side of torte.
reserved ⅓ cup whipped cream	Fill the pastry bag with whipped cream and make a rosette between each berry all around the outside edge.

Refrigerate the torte until serving.

Pfirsich-Cremetorte (peach cream torte)

Here is the perfect torte for an early summer day. It includes peaches bedded on a luscious *Quark*-cream. Whipped cream covers the torte, and peach slices, pistachios, and sliced almonds serve as the decoration.

9-inch basic spongecake (see master recipe, page 68)	Let the cake rest for a day before cutting it into 2 layers.

FILLING

⅔ cup whole milk ⅔ cup sugar 3 egg yolks	In a heavy saucepan, place milk, sugar, and egg yolks. With a wire whip, blend well together. Place on medium heat, constantly stirring the mixture. Boil slowly until thickened.
2 envelopes (2 tablespoons) unflavored, powdered gelatin 4-5 tablespoons good quality peach liqueur	In a separate saucepan or measuring cup, heat gelatin with the liqueur over medium heat until dissolved (do not boil). Stir dissolved gelatin into the egg mixture. Set aside to cool.
1 pint whipping cream 2 tablespoons sugar	Beat cream until stiff. Set aside.
2 cups *Quark* (see pages 149-151)	Beat *Quark* until smooth. Add the tepid egg-gelatin mixture to the *Quark* and blend well. With a wire whip, fold in half of the whipped cream, reserving the other half for the top and sides of the torte.

Place the peach cream into the refrigerator until thick enough to be spread. This will take about 1 to 1½ hours. While the cream is allowed to thicken, prepare the peaches. Use either fresh or canned peaches.

1½ pounds fresh peaches	Blanch the peaches for a few seconds in boiling water. Peel off the skin and remove the pit. A medium-size peach will give about 8 slices.
1½ pounds canned peaches	Drain peaches in a colander. Some slices may be too big, so divide them in two.

Leave 12 nice pieces of peach aside for the decoration on top. If you wish, cover the peach slices with peach liqueur. Drain again before using.

Assembling the Torte. Slice the spongecake horizontally (see page 75) and lay the top layer aside. With a spatula, spread half of the thickened peach cream on the bottom layer. Arrange the drained peach slices in a sunburst pattern. Cover with the rest of the cream. Carefully move the top layer onto it.

If you plan to freeze the torte, you may want to do so now with just the inside filling. It can be covered with whipped cream and decorated just before serving. (If you plan to do this, cut the whipped cream proportion above in half.)

With a long bladed knife, spread the reserved whipped cream evenly over the top and the sides, setting aside some for rosettes. Mark 12 pieces. Use a small star tube on the pastry bag, and place rosettes on the outside edge of each separate piece. Place a peach slice on each piece.

Several pistachios, chopped ½ cup sliced almonds, lightly toasted	Distribute the nuts in the center of the torte. Brush the sliced almonds over the whipped cream on the sides.

Refrigerate the torte for at least a few hours before serving so the peach cream can set completely.

Orangen-Weincreme-Torte (orange winecream torte)

People who are fond of *Weinschaum* (wine custard) will love this torte version of it. The custard is spread between layers of a spongecake, which is then covered with whipped cream and decorated with pieces of orange.

9-inch basic spongecake (see master recipe, page 68)	Let the cake rest for one day before cutting it into 3 layers.

FILLING

⅔ cup dry white wine ⅓ cup sugar grated peel of ½ lemon juice of ½ lemon juice of 2 oranges (about ½ cup) 4 egg yolks	In a simmering double boiler, combine wine, sugar, juice, and lemon peel. Add egg yolks one at a time, stirring vigorously with a wire whip. Beat for a few minutes until the mixture is lightly thickened. Take out of water bath and prepare the gelatin.
2 envelopes (2 tablespoons) powdered, unflavored gelatin 4 tablespoons water	In a small saucepan or measuring cup, dissolve gelatin with water over low heat. Keep 1 teaspoon of gelatin aside for the whipped cream. Blend the rest into the wine-egg mixture. Place into refrigerator to chill.
1 pint whipping cream 4 tablespoons confectioners sugar 2 tablespoons concentrated, frozen orange juice, thawed	Whip cream until stiff. Fold in the orange juice with a spatula.
reserved dissolved 1 teaspoon gelatin	If gelatin has hardened in the meantime, place over flame to soften again. Cool down until it is warm, and fold into the whipped cream with a spatula.

If the egg-wine mixture is cool (it should have the same temperature as whipped cream), fold one-half of the whipped cream into it, reserving the other half for the top and sides of the torte.

When the cream has been folded in (it is now called "winecream") it may still be fairly thin. Place it into the refrigerator for about 15 minutes, or until it thickens to spreading consistency.

In the meantime, slice the spongecake two times to make three layers, (see page 75).

12 orange slices	Prepare and set aside until needed.

Spread half of the winecream on the first layer. Cover with the second layer and spread on the rest of the cream. Replace top layer and cover top and sides with the remaining whipped cream. Mark 12 pieces on the top of torte. Decorate each with 1 slice of orange.

½ cup sliced, lightly toasted almonds	Brush the sides of torte with almonds, leaving a few for the center of the torte.

Refrigerate for a few hours before serving so the cream can set.

Heidelbeertorte (blueberry torte)

Since strawberries, peaches, or raspberries all go marvelously well with this *Quark* filling, you may substitute any of these fruits if they are in season and fresh.

9-inch basic spongecake, (see master recipe, page 68)	Allow the cake to rest for one day before cutting it into 2 layers.
1 pound (about 3 cups) blueberries	Wash blueberries and drain well in a colander.

FILLING

1 egg yolk	Beat egg yolk with sugar until light yellow in color. Add flavoring and *Quark*. Beat the mixture until smooth.
3 tablespoons sugar	
1 teaspoon vanilla extract	
grated peel of ½ lemon, if instead of blueberries you are using other fruit)	
1 cup *Quark*, pages 149-151	
2 teaspoons powdered, unflavored gelatin	In a measuring cup, dissolve gelatin with water over low heat. Cool until it is warm. Fold into the *Quark* mixture. Chill until thickened. In the meantime, prepare the whipped cream.
1½ tablespoons water	
½ pint whipping cream	Whip cream until stiff. Fold in the flavoring.
2 tablespoons confectioners sugar	
¼ teaspoon almond extract	
Or	
1-2 tablespoons kirsch, cognac, or rum	Fold 1 cup of whipped cream into the *Quark* mixture, reserving the other half for the sides of the torte.

Move bottom layer of cake onto a serving platter. Spread half of the cream on it. Move back top layer and spread on remainder. Distribute the berries, making one or two layers.

Gelatin glaze (master recipe, page 167)	Spoon the thickened gelatin over the fruit. Refrigerate for a while until gelatin has set.
reserved whipped cream	Spread cream on the sides of torte. If you wish, decorate with almond brittle.
1 cup *Krokant* (toasted almond brittle), page 170.	Brush over the cream.

Refrigerate the torte until serving.

Rehrücken (saddle of venison)

For a very special dinner, the Germans love *Rehrücken*—saddle of venison larded with bacon. Here is a torte which imitates in appearance this great dish.

The only requirement is a *Rehrücken* mold. This rectangular pan, about a foot long, is rounded and ribbed on the bottom so that the resulting cake resembles a real saddle of venison. It is available in many gourmet shops in this country.

The torte is covered with chocolate and finished with slivered almonds stuck in the icing to mimic the bacon lardons which lace the venison.

Preheat oven to 350°F.

12-inch long *Rehrücken* mold	Butter and sugar the mold.

BATTER

6 egg yolks	Beat egg yolks with the sugar, using Method III, page 65.
½ cup sugar	
grated peel of 1 lemon	Add lemon peel.
3 ounces finely ground, semisweet chocolate	Fold the chocolate into the egg-sugar mixture.
2½ cups finely ground filberts or unblanched almonds	
5 egg whites	In a separate bowl, beat the egg whites until stiff. With a wire whip, fold in half of the egg whites and nuts. Add remainder of the whites and fold in gently.

Immediately pour the batter into the prepared mold and bake in the middle of a preheated 350°F oven for 45 minutes, or until a cake tester inserted comes out clean (there may be a little chocolate hanging on the tester, so do not mistake it for batter). Let the cake rest for 5 minutes before unmolding it onto a cake rack.

Cool the torte completely before frosting it.

Chocolate butter frosting, page 165

½ cup slivered, blanched almonds

Pour frosting evenly over the torte. When it has set, decorate with the almonds. Stick in the points of almonds, about 3 or 4 in each rib, so they stand up.

Refrigerate until serving.

Serving Suggestion. A dollop of whipped cream goes very well with *Rehrücken*.

Prinzregententorte

Named after the Bavarian Prince Luitpold, this torte features a chocolate cream filling spread between eight layers of butter spongecake. Since the whole cake is covered with a chocolate frosting, the layers come as a surprise when it is first sliced.

There is no need to march out and buy eight layer pans in order to make this cake; instead, you can use one pan—a 9-inch springform pan or cake layer pan—as a model and manufacture your own duplicates out of heavy aluminum foil. It only takes a few minutes. Place the pan bottom on the foil and trace the circle with a pencil. Cut around this circle with scissors, going out about an inch for a rim. Turn up the rim and butter and flour the pan. Place the pan on a baking sheet before filling it with batter. With large enough baking sheets, you should be able to bake four layers at a time, two on each of two oven shelves.

Note: The faster the layers are baked, the better for the batter. If the batter has to sit while you laboriously bake one layer at a time, it will lose its fluffiness. If that is the only way you can do it, however, I would suggest dividing the recipe and beating two separate batters.

Preheat oven to 375°F.

BATTER

7 egg whites
1¼ cups sugar
pinch of salt
1 tablespoon lemon juice
grated peel of ½ lemon
7 egg yolks
1⅔ cups sifted cake flour
½ cup (1 stick) unsalted butter, melted

See page 66 for preparing the butter spongecake.

Immediately spread with a spatula a thin layer of batter in the first prepared pans which have been set on baking sheets. Store the rest of the batter in the refrigerator until needed again. Bake in a preheated 375°F oven for about 12 minutes or until the layers are a light golden color.

When baked, unmold at once, turning the pan upside down on a cake rack, peeling off the foil. Stack the layers with a piece of wax paper or baking parchment between them so they will not stick together. While still warm, place a board or pan on top of the layers to prevent the sides from curling up. Choose the most perfect layer for the top. Stacked with paper between them, they may be stored for a day or frozen.

Chocolate Buttercream with Custard Base, page 153
Or
either of the Parisian Creams, page 156
Chocolate Butter Frosting, double recipe, page 165

Spread about 3 tablespoons of chocolate cream on each layer, setting them on top of each other. Leave the top layer plain for the frosting.

Spread frosting evenly over the top and sides of torte. Let it set completely before slicing.

Dobos Torte

This specialty originated in Budapest, but it has been borrowed by the rest of Europe. It is a many-layered cake (this version has eight), filled with chocolate buttercream and covered with an unusual topping: shiny caramel!

9-inch springform pan or cake layer pan

See previous recipe, *Prinzregententorte*, for instructions on how to make 8 layer pans.

Preheat oven to 375°F.

BATTER

7 egg whites
1¼ cups sugar
pinch of salt
1 tablespoon lemon juice
grated peel of ½ lemon
7 egg yolks
1½ cups sifted cake flour

Use Method I, page 64, for preparing the spongecake.

For baking and unmolding the layers, see *Prinzregententorte*.

CHOCOLATE BUTTERCREAM

3 ounces semisweet chocolate
1 ounce unsweetened chocolate
1 cup (2 sticks) unsalted butter, softened
1 cup confectioners sugar
1 tablespoon rum
4 tablespoons whipping cream
2 egg yolks

Melt chocolate in a double boiler over barely simmering water. Set aside to cool.

Beat the butter until fluffy. Add the sugar slowly. When well blended, beat in the rum. Continue beating and add the cream by spoonfuls.

Add the egg yolks. The mixture should be fluffy and light.
Beat in the cooled chocolate.

Set aside the top layer for the caramel topping, placing it on a sheet of foil so it will be easy to move once the topping is on. Spread the remaining seven layers each with about three tablespoons of buttercream, ending with a top layer of cream. There should be some left for the side of the torte.

Place the torte in the refrigerator while completing the caramel topping.

CARAMEL TOPPING

Before you start, prepare a basin with cold water to cool the hot saucepan. Have on hand a sharp knife with a buttered blade.	In a heavy-bottomed saucepan or iron skillet, melt 1 cup of sugar over medium heat. Stir with a wooden spoon or metal spatula until the sugar is completely melted and has turned a caramel brown. Dip the saucepan in the cold water for an instant to stop further cooking. Pour at once over the top of the cake layer.

With the buttered knife, deeply score the caramel as if slicing a cake. This has to be done immediately since the caramel hardens almost at once. When the caramel is hard and cool, take the layer, which rests on a piece of foil, and set on top of the torte. When the torte is served, just slice through the scored pieces.

reserved buttercream	Spread buttercream around the side of the torte.
½ cup sliced almonds, lightly toasted.	Brush almonds over the buttercream.

Marzipantorte (almond paste torte)

There is no particularly traditional way for making a *Marzipan Torte*. You may completely cover a butter spongecake with rolled-out almond paste, or cover only the top and brush the sides with sliced almonds. Spread a very thin layer of chocolate butter frosting over it, just barely enough to coat it, otherwise it will detract from the delicate taste of the marzipan. Decoration can be marzipan pieces, chocolates, and whole, halved, or sliced almonds.

9-inch Butter Spongecake	The cake should be thoroughly cooled and set on a serving platter.
1 cup apricot preserves, page 166	Brush the cake with hot preserves.
1 cup marzipan (almond paste), page 171	Use a Formica top or marble slab as a working area when rolling out almond paste. Dust the working area lightly with confectioners sugar. Roll out the marzipan about ⅛ inch thick, trying to roll a circle. Place a 9-inch pan on top of the circle as a guide. Draw a circle around with a sharp

knife. Loosen almond paste carefully from the working area with a long bladed knife. Cut the circle in half (it is too difficult to move the whole round without breaking). Slip a piece of wax paper under the first half and move on top of the torte. Follow with the other half and combine them with your fingers. Bend over hanging sides downward. Roll out the rest of the almond paste in long strips. Measure the height of your torte and cut out strips accordingly. Cut them about 3 to 4 inches long and place them around the sides, combining them with the top and with each other.

Chocolate butter frosting, page 165, without additional flavor

Pour a thin layer of frosting over the torte, just enough so the almond paste does not show through any more. Let the frosting set before slicing the torte.

Zitronentorte (lemon torte)

A spongecake can always be filled with a lemon buttercream, but I like even more this interesting recipe with its extra "lemony" taste. The torte may be coated either with whipped cream or with one of the lemon frostings given at the end of the recipe.

9-inch Butter Spongecake

Flavor the spongecake batter with the grated peel of 1 lemon. Let the cake rest for one day before cutting it into 3 layers.

LEMON CREAM (*About 1 ½ cups*):

½ cup (1 stick) unsalted butter
⅔ cup sugar
grated peel of 1 lemon
juice of 2 lemons
5 egg yolks

In a heavy saucepan, over low heat, melt butter. Stir in the sugar with a wire whip. When well blended, add lemon juice and peel. Add egg yolks one at a time and beat until the mixture is thick and coats a spoon. Chill to spreading consistency.

Move the bottom layer onto a serving platter and spread with one-half of the lemon cream. Add the second layer, spread on the rest of the cream, and replace the top layer.

Frosting the Zitronentorte. Here are three possibilities:

I. Whipped Cream
½ pint whipping cream
2 tablespoons confectioners sugar
grated peel of ½ lemon

Whip cream until stiff. Fold in lemon peel.

Spread whipped cream evenly over top and sides of the torte, leaving some aside for decoration. Mark 12 or 16 pieces on top of the torte to serve as a guide. Fill a pastry bag and decorate to your liking with the leftover whipped cream. Lightly toasted nuts may also be used for special accents.

II. Lemon fondant (master recipe, pages 161-162) with 3 tablespoons lemon juice, strained	If the torte is to receive an icing, move it to a wire rack. Spread icing evenly over it and let set completely before slicing.
III. Lemon icing, page 164	

Sachertorte

My guess is that the original recipe for this torte lies in a locked drawer of the Hotel Sacher in Vienna—as well it should! Of all the various attempts to plagiarize this famous cake, I like this one best.

Preheat oven to 375°F.	
8-inch springform pan	Butter and flour the pan.
4 ounces semisweet chocolate	Melt chocolate in a double boiler over barely simmering water. Set aside to cool
½ ounce unsweetened chocolate	

BATTER

½ cup plus 2 tablespoons unsalted butter	Cream butter, sugar, and egg yolks, using one of the methods on pages 11-13
⅞ cup sugar	
6 egg yolks	
big pinch of grated lemon peel	Add the flavorings.
big pinch of cinnamon	
pinch of salt	
melted chocolate as above	Beat chocolate slowly in the butter-egg mixture. Chocolate should be no more than warm. Continue beating for several minutes until the mixture again looks light and fluffy.
⅞ cup sifted cake flour	Fold in the flour.
6 egg whites	Beat egg whites separately and fold in delicately.

Pour immediately into the prepared pan and bake on the lowest rack of a preheated 375°F oven for 45 minutes, or until a cake tester inserted in the center comes out clean. Let the cake cool 10 minutes before turning out onto a cake rack to cool thoroughly.

The torte should be allowed to rest for one day before filling and frosting it.

Slice the cake horizontally into two layers, page 75.

1½ cups apricot preserves, page 166.
Spread ⅔ cup of preserves on bottom layer. Move top layer back and brush the entire outside of the torte with rest of glaze. Let dry.

Chocolate sugar frosting (master recipe, page 164).
Set the torte on a wire rack and pour frosting evenly over it.

Serving Suggestion. *Sachertorte* is customarily served with a spoonful of whipped cream next to it on the plate.

Brandteig

(cream puff pastry)

The dough for cream puff pastry is cooked on top of the stove before being baked in the oven. The fluffy puff of pastry produced serves as a shell for a variety of fillings—either for a sweet dessert or with a cheese or meat filling for elegant hors d'oeuvres. Cream puffs require but little work; they can be made in separate steps. They always look festive and taste heavenly.

Cream Puff Pastry Dough

½ cup (1 stick) unsalted butter
1 cup water
pinch of salt
1¼ cups sifted flour
4 eggs

With a wire whip, combine butter, salt, and water in a heavy saucepan over medium heat. Once the butter has melted, bring to a boil and add all of the flour at once. Beat the mixture vigorously until well blended. Turn the heat to low and continue beating until the dough no longer sticks to the whip or the bottom and sides of the pan. The dough will now look glossy and be rather stiff.

Remove the dough to a large mixing bowl. By hand or with a mixer, blend in the eggs one at a time, waiting for each to be very well incorporated before dropping in the next. When all the eggs are added, the dough should look soft, glossy, and golden in color; and when it is lifted with a whip, it should fall back heavily, holding its shape. Be cautious, however: Before adding the fourth egg, carefully examine the dough. Slight variations in flour quality and egg size can make a considerable difference. You may therefore wish to add only half of the fourth egg or add yet another half an egg after the fourth, depending on how heavy the dough is.

At this point the dough may be kept for one or two days in the refrigerator.

Cream Puffs. The dough may be dropped on a lightly buttered baking sheet, either by using a pastry bag equipped with a large, round tube opening, or by using two large tablespoons periodically dipped in cold water. Press the dough into little mounds, or shape into large rosettes about 2 inches in diameter. Remember that the puffs will expand in the oven, so leave them about 2 inches apart.

Eclairs. This shape cannot be produced very successfully without the help of a pastry bag. Squeeze out onto a lightly buttered baking sheet two parallel rows of dough, touching each other, about 5 inches long. Squeeze another two rows on top of these, making a block of four rows. Leave 2 inches between each eclair.

Baking the Cream Puff Pastry

Puffs and eclairs should be baked in a fairly hot oven. Place the baking sheet in the middle of a 450°F preheated oven and bake for about 15 to 20 minutes, or until they are light brown. You may test one puff by opening it to see if it is cooked all the way through. It may steam, but it should not show visible moisture.

Note: Do not open the oven door for the first 15 minutes. If the puffs have not formed a crust, cool air will make them fall and they will not rise again.

Out of the oven, place the baking sheet in a draft-free place. Let cool for a few minutes and then move the puffs to a wire rack to cool completely.

Storing the Puffs

The freshly baked puffs should be served soon. When they sit for a time, the crust loses its crispness and they tend to become soggy. They can, however, be very successfully frozen before they are filled. When the puffs are still warm, place into the freezer. To restore crispness, place frozen puffs in a preheated 400°F oven for about 8 minutes, or until they are crisp.

Filled cream puffs are best when eaten shortly after they have been filled. Be sure to refrigerate until serving.

Windbeutel (cream puffs)

Literally translated, a *Windbeutel* is a "windbag," but you won't confuse our English conception of "a talkative bore" with these delights of German bakery art! While they are traditionally filled with whipped cream flavored with rum or kirsch, you may also set your imagination at work to create fillings of vanilla or chocolate cream, or whipped cream mixed with puréed or whole fruit such as raspberries and strawberries.

Basic cream puff pastry, page 101
1 pint (2 cups) whipping cream, flavored with rum or kirsch
Or
2 cups buttercream with custard base, page 153
Or
Vanilla cream, page 154

With a sharp knife, cut ⅓ off each puff for the top.
Fill the cream into a pastry bag equipped with a ribbon tube. Fill each puff with a generous amount of cream.

Dust each puff with confectioners sugar. Refrigerate until serving. This recipe will make about 15 cream puffs.

Mokkaschnitten (eclairs)

Whereas Americans tend to prepare their eclairs with a vanilla custard filling and chocolate topping, Germans make them with coffee-flavored cream (using whipped cream, custard, or custard based buttercream) frosted with coffee fondant or simple sugar icing. For a change consider also the mocha filling on page 154 and dust the top with confectioners sugar.

Basic cream puff pastry, page 101
1 cup coffee-flavored fondant, page 161
Or
1 cup coffee-flavored simple sugar icing, page 164

1 pint (2 cups) whipping cream, coffee-flavored
Or
2 cups buttercream with custard base, coffee-flavored, page 153
Or
Vanilla cream, page 154 flavored with
2-3 teaspoons powdered instant coffee

With a sharp knife, cut each eclair in half.

Ice each top and replace on eclair after icing has hardened.

Fill the cream into a pastry bag equipped with a ribbon tube opening. Fill each puff with a generous amount of cream.

Place the iced top gently on top of the filling.

Refrigerate until serving. This recipe will make about 14 eclairs.

Brandteig

Strudel

Despite its great popularity in Germany, especially in Bavaria, there is nothing uniquely German about strudel. In fact, I got my first lesson in strudel making not in Germany but from my Czechoslovakian neighbor, Mrs. Jitka Mencik, an expert cook and strudel maker.

The dough itself is actually a simple noodle dough made more elastic by the addition of a small amount of butter or oil. Once stretched out to a very thin leaf, it is wrapped around a delicious filling. In the oven the leaves of dough puff up slightly and the top layers become crisp and flaky. Strudel can be served warm or cold, with a generous dusting of confectioners sugar.

Preparing the Baking Sheet. A baking sheet with sides is preferable, since the fruit juices sometimes find their way out of the strudel. You may line a straight baking sheet with aluminum foil and turn up the sides for the same effect. Butter the sheet or foil generously.

Strudel Dough

1¾ cups unbleached flour
1 egg
2 tablespoons unsalted butter, melted and cooled until it is warm
pinch of salt
½ cup water, tepid

For basting:
6 tablespoons unsalted butter, melted

Measure the flour into a big bowl. Make a well in the center of the flour and add the egg, salt, and melted butter. With a fork or spatula stir the liquid ingredients, gradually incorporating some flour into the mixture. Slowly add one-third cup of water and continue mixing. Take it out of the bowl and place on a floured working surface. Start kneading with the palm of your hand, occasionally adding still more water; you may need an additional 2 to 4 tablespoons. In case the dough is too wet and sticks to hands and surface, carefully add more flour. Keep kneading the dough until it is elastic but rather dry, and soft to the touch, "as soft," so my teacher says, "as a baby's bottom." Occasionally stop kneading and throw the dough repeatedly and forcefully against the working surface. This violent treatment, though unkind, will soften the dough and make for a shorter kneading time. As you knead, the dough will blister, and these air bubbles indicate elasticity and stretchability. The entire kneading time should be about 15 to 20 minutes. Finally, give the dough a light overall coating of flour and cover it with a warm inverted bowl. It should rest for a half an hour (do not let it sit for more than an hour, otherwise the outside may dry and the dough lose its elasticity).

Using a Mixer. The use of a heavy-duty mixer for such a simple dough (a hand-held mixer would be too weak to work) would only be worthwhile if you were making several strudels at the same time, or if you were using part of the dough for noodle making. Should you decide to use the machine, prepare everything as with the hand method. After the water has been kneaded in, I would recommend continuing to work by hand in order to have the right feel for the consistency of the dough.

Stretching the Dough

While the dough is resting, prepare the table. It should be about 3 feet square. Spread a table cloth (or your special pastry cloth) over it. Lightly dust the cloth with flour and set the ball of dough in the center of it. Brush the dough with melted butter and roll it out with a rolling pin. When it is as thin as you can make it with the rolling pin, dust your hands with flour and start stretching by hand. Working from the center outward, gently lift up and pull at the dough with your fingers until it stretches a bit. Walking around the table, repeat this gentle stretching all around. Be discrete and resist the urge to give the dough anything more than gentle tugs; you will find that it stretches very satisfactorily. Continue pulling and stretching, trying to keep the dough in the center of the table so it can be pulled evenly all around. Stretch it until it is transparently thin, so thin that—as most strudel making instruction books advise—a newspaper can be read through it. If, despite all your care, a hole shows up, brush around it with melted butter and patch with some dough from the outside. Never try to press the entire dough together and start from the beginning as it dries out while being stretched and tends to lose its elasticity. Finally, trim the thick edges from the outside, leaving a single transparent sheet of dough.

Filling and Rolling the Dough

Brush the entire dough with melted butter. Spread half of the bread crumbs (sautéed in butter, if you wish) on the half of the dough nearest you. Over this goes the fruit, then the sugar, chopped nuts if you are using them, spices, raisins, and finally the other half of the bread crumbs. Lifting the edge of the tablecloth to "start things rolling," roll up the filled part of the strudel first, ending with the unfilled dough. The final layers of unfilled dough will securely wrap the filling and puff up to a crisp outside. Pinch together the ends of the strudel or fold them under. Now place the prepared baking sheet next to the strudel and with the help of the cloth roll it on to the sheet. Curve the strudel into the horseshoe shape. Brush with melted butter and bake immediately.

Baking the Strudel

The oven temperature should be fairly hot at first. Bake at 425°F on the lower middle rack of the oven for the first 10 minutes. Then turn it down to 375°F and bake for another 35 minutes, or until the strudel is crisp and golden brown. Halfway through the baking, brush the surface again with melted butter.

When it is out of the oven, baste the strudel a third time with a little more melted butter. Let cool until it is warm, then dust with confectioners sugar.

Leftover or frozen strudel may be reheated in a 400°F oven for about 10 to 15 minutes.

Each strudel yields about twelve 2-inch slices.

Apfelstrudel (apple strudel)

If a poll were taken to identify the most popular strudel, apple strudel would win hands down.

14 x 16-inch baking sheet	Butter the sheet.
Basic strudel dough, pages 105-106	
	FILLING
1½ cups good-quality, fresh bread crumbs	
3 pounds tart, crisp apples (about 9 cups sliced)	Peel and core apples. Cut into quarter-inch thick slices. Toss the apples with lemon juice.
2 tablespoons lemon juice (optional)	
½ cup sugar	Fill and roll the dough, then bake as directed on pages 106-107.
1 teaspoon cinnamon	
1 cup sultanas or raisins	
½ cup sliced almonds or medium-ground filberts or walnuts	

Birnenstrudel (pear strudel)

Substitute 3 pounds pears for apples and proceed as in the apple strudel recipe.

Rhabarberstrudel (rhubarb strudel)

14 x 16-inch baking sheet Butter the sheet.
Basic strudel dough,
    pages 105-106

FILLING

1½ cups good-quality, fresh
    bread crumbs
2½ pounds fresh rhubarb Wash rhubarb. Cut woody ends off. Slice
    (about 7 cups sliced)   into ½ inch pieces.
1½ cups sugar Fill and roll the dough, then bake as
1 cup coarsely chopped   directed on page 107.
    walnuts or filberts

Zwetschgenstrudel (prune plum strudel)

14 x 16-inch baking sheet Butter the sheet.
Basic strudel dough,
    pages 105-106

FILLING

1½ cups good-quality, fresh
    bread crumbs
3 pounds prune plums Cut each plum in half. Take out the pit and
    (about 7 cups quartered)   quarter each slice.
1 cup sugar Fill and roll the dough, then bake
½ cup sliced almonds   as directed on page 107.

Kirschenstrudel (cherry strudel)

14 x 16-inch baking sheet Butter the sheet.
Basic strudel dough,
    pages 105-106

FILLING

1½ cups good-quality, fresh
    bread crumbs
3 pounds pitted cherries, If using frozen or canned cherries, drain well
    fresh, frozen, or canned   in a colander.
    (about 7 cups)
½ cup sugar Fill and roll the dough, then bake
1 teaspoon cinnamon   as directed on page 107.
1 cup medium-ground almonds
    or filberts

Quarkstrudel

14 x 16-inch baking sheet	Butter the sheet.
Basic strudel dough, pages 105-106	

FILLING

½ cup (1 stick) unsalted butter, softened	Cream the soft butter until light and fluffy. Add sugar and egg yolks.
¾ cup sugar	
2 egg yolks	
3 tablespoons sour cream	Mix in sour cream, flavoring, and *Quark*.
1 teaspoon vanilla extract Or	
grated peel of ½ lemon	
3 cups *Quark,* pages 149-151	

Spread the filling over half of the buttered strudel leaf and continue as described on pages 106-107.

Blätterteig

(puff pastry)

Hundreds of thin layers or "leaves" *(Blätter)* of dough sandwiched between layers of butter are the secret of this wonderful pastry. Butter and steam caught between the layers helps them to puff up. This is what gives this light, tender, crisp pastry its characteristic profile. It can be used as part of a first-course delicacy, as the crust for Beef Wellington, or in its various forms it can be the basis for a fine dessert. France in particular has produced some great dishes using this pastry.

I was delighted finally to learn the technique for making it myself. There is no reason to hesitate trying it if you follow the simple rules and recipe step by step.

Puff Pastry Dough

In preparing puff pastry, there are a few important things to remember:

Do not attempt to make puff pastry in hot weather if you do not have an air-conditioned kitchen. The dough should be kept cold during all the "turns"—the separate rollings of the dough. In case the dough softens from working on it too long at room temperature, place it back into the refrigerator to chill.

About 5 hours are needed to ready puff pastry dough for baking. But during this time you are only working on the dough for a little more than half an hour; the rest of the time is taken up by the dough's "rest periods." The rest periods should not be shortened, since the dough needs to be cold and the gluten in the flour must relax between the turns. Otherwise the dough will not extend itself sufficiently while being rolled. The rest period after the fourth turn can, however, be delayed. After the dough has had its sixth turn, you may either chill it for 2 hours before shaping, resting it again and finally baking it, or keep it in the refrigerator for several days. At this point, puff pastry dough may also be frozen for months.

The consistency of flour makes a big difference in preparing the dough. Hard wheat flour mixed with some soft wheat flour is preferable. I am very satisfied with the results of unbleached all-purpose flour (which is higher in gluten content) mixed with the bleached all-purpose flour. If you cannot find unbleached flour, use only the other variety. Cake flour, which is very low in gluten, is not recommended for this type of dough. The gluten in the flour makes for an elastic dough, which is necessary so that the alternate layers of butter do not break through when the dough is rolled out.

Other recipes for puff pastry may instruct one to knead water out of the butter. This is unnecessary if you are using unsalted butter. While kneading and shaping the butter sticks together in the form of a brick, the butter should not be too cold, not too soft. The finished brick of butter ought to have about the same consistency as the dough, so the two can be successfully rolled out together.

This dough does not contain any sugar. When it is used for sweet desserts it is often encrusted with sugar, which turns into a light caramel coating in the oven.

Puff pastry needs to be baked in a hot oven. Once it has risen, turn the temperature down somewhat, according to the individual recipe.

Note: Several puff pastry recipes ask for beaten egg. Place the egg into a bowl and add 1 to 2 teaspoons water. Beat with a fork until the white and yellow of the egg are well combined.

About Thawing Frozen, Already Baked Puff Pastry. Place pastry on a baking sheet. Leave for a few minutes in a 375°F preheated oven, then turn oven off and leave about 10 minutes longer.

DOUGH MIXTURE

2 cups bleached flour
2 cups unbleached flour
1¼ cups water
2 egg yolks
¼ teaspoon salt
2 cups (4 sticks) unsalted butter

Blend the two kinds of flour together in a bowl. Reserve 3 tablespoons of flour for the butterbrick. Make a well in the center of the flour and pour in about two-thirds of the water. Add egg yolks and salt. With a spatula, mix egg yolks and water, then work in the flour. Take the mixture out of the bowl and place on a floured working surface. Start kneading with the palm of your hand, cautiously adding more water. Be very careful in adding water: if too much is used, you will have to add more flour, which will bring the amounts of butter and flour out of proportion. Knead the dough about 15 minutes until it is very elastic, smooth in consistency and soft—very much like a strudel dough. Shape the dough into a ball, flour lightly, wrap in wax paper, and seal in plastic to prevent drying out. Let rest in the refrigerator for 30 minutes.

Using a Heavy-Duty Mixer. Place ingredients into the bowl as described. Knead with the dough hook, and when dough clings in a large mass around the hook and no longer sticks to sides of bowl, allow the machine to run about 5 to 7 minutes longer. Take out of bowl and see if dough has the right consistency. If necessary, knead a while longer.

While the dough is resting, prepare the butter. Place the sticks of cold butter next to each other. Fuse them together by kneading with the knuckles of your fingers. Shape the whole into a 6-inch square brick, 1-inch thick. While kneading, the butter will get softer, but should still feel cold and have about the same consistency as the dough. Coat the whole butterbrick with the reserved 3 tablespoons of flour and pat the flour into the brick.

Remove the dough from the refrigerator and place on a well-floured working surface, such as a cloth or marble slab. Roll out four sides like petals from the ball-shaped dough. The inner part of the dough should be slightly thicker, about one-third inch thick and a bit larger than the butterbrick. The petals should measure one-quarter inch thick. Brush off excess flour and place the butter at the center of the dough. Fold petals over the butter (avoid stretching) so that the butter is completely enclosed. Seal the edges with your fingers. You now have a pretty "package" of butter, well wrapped in dough.

Turns 1 and 2. Dust the working surface as well as the top of the dough package with flour. Turn the package upside down so that seams are on the bottom. With an even motion, rolling away from you, roll out the dough to a rectangle, 20 inches long and 8 inches wide. During this procedure, the butter inside the dough will be evenly distributed between the two dough layers. Fold the bottom third of dough up to the center, then fold the top third down to meet the center to make three even layers (exactly like folding a letter). Always brush off excess flour after rolling and folding the separate layers.

Now give the dough a quarter turn counterclockwise so that the top flap is on your right, facing you like a book.

Again roll the dough into a rectangle, 20 x 8 inches in size. Then fold again in three even parts, as previously done. Remember or note down on a piece of paper that you have now completed two turns. Dust dough with flour, wrap in wax paper and a plastic bag, and refrigerate for 30 minutes. The butter layers are still fairly thick between the dough layers. It is therefore advisable not to chill the dough longer, otherwise the butter may become too hard. If this does happen, beat the dough lightly with the rolling pin until the butter is softened enough to be rolled.

Turns 3 and 4. Repeat these two rollings and foldings of dough exactly as in turns 1 and 2. It is important that the dough is turned counterclockwise and have the top flap with its open side on the right every time before rerolling the dough. After the fourth turn, let the wrapped dough rest for 60 minutes or longer if you wish.

Turns 5 and 6. Use the same method as for the previous turns. Let the wrapped dough rest for 2 hours before shaping and baking it. Or you may keep it for several days in the refrigerator; it can at this point be frozen for months.

About Leftover Dough. Scraps of leftover dough can be easily "recycled" for uses that do not require the pastry to rise very much, like lining tartlet molds or making cut-outs for decoration.

If any large pieces of dough are left, place them neatly against each other. Moisten the edges of the scraps and roll over them gently with the rolling pin. This way they may satisfactorily combine. Chill the dough for 1 hour before shaping it.

If they do not combine well, or only small scraps are available, use the following method. Arrange pieces in rectangular shape. Roll over them to combine, then fold in three layers as in turn 1 when the dough was first made. Chill for an hour, roll and fold, making a second turn. Chill again, then shape the dough.

Blätterteigboden für Obstkuchen (puff pastry shell for tarts)

A tender, crisp puff pastry shell, filled with fruit, whipped cream, or custard is wonderful for a festive table. This recipe makes two 10-inch tart shells.

10-inch springform pan ½ recipe puff pastry, page 111

Roll out the dough to one-eighth inch thick on a floured surface. Place the 10-inch pan on top as a guide, and cut a circle with a pastry wheel or knife. From that cut, measure out 2 inches all around (if you happen to have a 14-inch round guide, use it). Cut the second circle, forming a 2-inch circular strip with an outside diameter of 14 inches. This strip is intended to make the side of the tart shell.

Rinse the bottom of the 10-inch springform pan with water (do not dry), wrap dough around rolling pin, and place into the pan bottom. Assemble the pan. Moisten the pan sides and the outside edge of the bottom dough with water. Now take the circle intended for the sides and, since it is difficult to manipulate it whole, cut into two equal parts. Combine it around the edge of the bottom dough using your fingers or the back of a fork, overlapping the two pieces. If the pastry slips from the side of the pan, moisten the side again to make the dough more adhesive.

Prick the bottom of the pastry with a fork at one-quarter-inch intervals. Place a lightly buttered 9-inch pan into the dough-lined pan, or butter a piece of aluminum foil or baking parchment and fill with dried beans for the same effect. This will weight down the pastry, keeping the bottom from puffing up and supporting the sides so they will not collapse during baking. Chill the dough-lined pan for 30 minutes.

Bake in a 425°F preheated oven for 15 to 20 minutes, or until the sides of pastry show a light browning. Remove the inner pan or beans with paper and bake the shell for another 5 minutes or so. The shell should look uniformly, nicely browned.

Cool for 5 minutes to allow pastry to shrink from the pan sides. With a knife, carefully loosen shell from sides, open the pan sides, and unmold onto a wire rack.

Note: Tartlets made from puff pastry dough may be shaped and baked in the same manner as a large tart shell.

Fillings for Puff Pastry Shells. Use any of the fillings designed for tarts (made from rich tart pastry), usually a fully baked shell.

Fill the tart and serve it shortly thereafter, or freeze the tart shell.

Gefüllter Blätterkuchen (covered puff pastry tart)

Two sheets of puff pastry filled with applesauce—a very easily made dessert. This produces about twelve 1¼ inch slices.

½ recipe puff pastry, page 111
14 x 16-inch baking sheet   Rinse sheet with water but do not dry.

Divide dough in half. Place one half in the refrigerator. Dust the working surface with flour and roll the other half into a rectangle, 16 inches long, 8 inches wide, and one-eighth inch thick. Roll the dough over the rolling pin and transfer to the prepared baking sheet. Prick the entire surface with a fork at one-quarter-inch intervals.

⅓ cup apricot preserves   Spread the jam on the dough within a border of ¾ inch all around.

1½ to 2 cups thick, homemade applesauce, page 57. Use ½ recipe and omit sultanas.   Cover the jam with applesauce. Chill the filled dough for 20 minutes.

Moisten the dough border with water. Roll out the second half of the dough, about one-half inch larger all around than the first piece. Place on top of the filled dough. With the back of a fork, press the borders together; this fuses them and gives a design which looks nice when the pastry is baked. Cover the pastry with wax paper and chill again for 30 minutes.

Preheat oven to 450°F. Brush the tart with beaten egg. With a sharp knife, make a number of slashes across the top of the tart where you will wish eventually to cut it. Brush again with egg.

Place in the lower middle of a 450°F oven for 15 or 20 minutes, until the pastry has puffed and starts to brown. Then turn down heat to 375°F for another 25 or 30 minutes. In case the pastry turns too brown on the top, cover lightly with aluminum foil. This tart needs a long baking period so that all the layers of the pastry can be baked through.

Serving Suggestions. Serve the tart warm or cold, plain or with whipped cream. It tastes best, however, when eaten on the same day it is baked. Or you may freeze it.

Variations. Use any other preserves for the filling or any cooked fruit you like.

Tausend-Blätter-Torte (thousand layer torte)

Bake either four, six, or eight layers, depending on how high you want the torte to be. There are a number of choices for fillings.

For 4 layers, each 9 inches
    in diameter
½ recipe puff pastry, page 111
2 large baking sheets   Rinse baking sheets with water but do not dry.

Place half the dough, which will be used to make two disks, on a floured working surface. Roll out the dough to 18 or 19 inches long, 9 to 10 inches wide, and one-eighth inch thick. Place a 9-inch round pan on top of dough and draw a circle with a knife or pastry wheel. Transfer the shaped dough to a prepared baking sheet. With a fork, prick the dough over the entire surface, going all the way through, about one-quarter inch apart. Chill for 30 minutes. Repeat the procedure with second half of the dough. If you have some scraps left over, make little cut-outs in the shapes of flowers or stars and set these decoratively on top of one of the rounds. Use this round as the top layer when you finish the torte.

Preheat oven to 450°F. Before baking, glaze each round of dough with beaten egg. Place on the middle rack of the oven and bake each layer for about 12 minutes, or until the pastry has puffed and browned. Unmold onto a cake rack.

Use the same day for a torte, or freeze.

1 cup apricot preserves, page 166	Brush the preserves on to the 3 layers and the top layer as well if it is to be iced.
Vanilla cream with whipped cream, page 154. It may also be flavored with rum, kirsch, or cognac	Spread on each layer about ⅔ cup of cream. Place decorated layer on top. You may want to precut the top layer in serving pieces and place them separately next to each other, since the torte is a little difficult to slice when sandwiched together. With rest of cream, cover the sides of torte.
½ cup pistachio nuts, chopped Or ½ cup sliced almonds	Brush nuts over the cream.

Refrigerate the torte, but leave at room temperature for a while before serving. Cut or saw with a very sharp, hot knife into 8 slices.

Variations. You may fill the torte with flavored whipped cream, using 1 pint of whipping cream. If there is no decoration on the top layer, ice it with 1 cup of rum or lemon frosting of your choice.

Schillerlocken (cream horns)

The German name (literally, "Schiller's locks") pays sweet homage to Swabia's great romantic poet.

22 cone-shaped tubes (Ladylock Sticks) 5½ inches long. There are also smaller tubes on the market. If you use smaller ones, make dough strips a couple of inches shorter.	Butter the tubes well.
2 large baking sheets	Rinse sheets with water but do not dry.

For 20 to 22 cream horns:
½ recipe puff pastry, page 111

On a well-floured surface, roll out the dough to a rectangle 22 inches long and 17 to 18 inches wide. Trim off the ragged edges of the dough. With a sharp knife or pastry wheel cut out strips along the width, 1 inch wide and 17 to 18 inches long. Use a ruler as a guide to make the strips straight. Hold the tube at the large opening and start on the other side to slip the dough around in a circle on the outside of the tube. Pinch dough together at the seam. From there, wind dough around clockwise in spiral form up to the large opening, overlapping the edges on each wind by one-eighth inch. There will be approximately 6 turns on a 5½-inch-long tube. Leave about one-half inch of the tube without dough at the large end so that the baked pastry can be easily slipped off. Do not stretch the dough while wrapping around the tube, or it will shrink and break while baking.

Place each mold on the baking sheet, seam down. Allow to rest for 30 to 60 minutes in the refrigerator to relax dough and prevent shrinking in the oven.

1 egg, beaten with 1 teaspoon water	Preheat oven to 425°F. Before baking the pastry, brush each dough-wrapped tube lightly with egg. Avoid, however, brushing it on the bottom (which is the seam side), since the egg would function as an adhesive to the baking sheet.
Granulated or crystallized sugar	Roll in sugar, again avoiding the bottom of dough.

Bake on the middle rack of a preheated 425°F oven for 10 minutes. Then turn down heat to 375°F for another 5 to 10 minutes, or until the pastry looks nicely browned.

Out of the oven, loosen the pastry immediately from the baking sheet. Then take each horn from its tube with a twisting motion. This must be done while the pastry is still hot. Fill after the horns have cooled.

1 pint whipping cream, flavored with vanilla	Place whipped cream into a pastry bag and squeeze cream into each horn. Serve *Schillerlocken* soon after filling.

Blätterteig

Aprikosenrädchen (apricot windmills)

Kleinbäckerei (small pastries) made from puff pastry come in an endless variety of shapes. Apricot windmills and nut combs are just two of the fun ones.

For 10 to 12 pieces of pastry:
½ recipe puff pastry, page 111 and some left over dough scraps if available.
2 large baking sheets — Rinse sheets with water but do not dry.
1-pound can apricot halves — Drain the fruit well in a colander.

On a floured working surface, roll out the dough to a three-sixteenths-inch-thick rectangle, 20 inches long and 15 inches wide. Cut out twelve 5-inch squares with a pastry wheel or knife. Set each square on a prepared baking sheet, holding aside two squares for the top of apricot halves (this is unnecessary if you have dough scraps on hand). Chill the dough for 30 minutes.

Roll out the two reserved squares again, to about one-eighth inch thick. Cut out rounds about 2 inches in diameter so that they will cover the fruit. Prick those rounds several times with a fork and place in the refrigerator to chill.

Preheat oven to 450°F. Brush each dough square with beaten egg, not quite up to the edges (otherwise dough may not rise there satisfactorily). Set in the center of each square one apricot half. Make a diagonal cut from each corner of the square up to the fruit. Twist each of the four resulting flaps of dough to make a windmill blade. Place a dough round on the apricot half. Brush the entire pastry lightly again with beaten egg.

Bake on the middle rack of a 450°F preheated oven for 15 minutes, then turn heat down to 400°F and bake for another 5 to 10 minutes, or until the pastry has browned. With a spatula, unmold immediately onto a wire rack.

While the pastry is baking, prepare the icing.

1 cup apricot preserves, page 166
½ cup confectioners sugar
1 egg white

With a brush, apply icing while pastry is still hot.
Beat until well combined. The mixture should be fairly thin. Brush over entire pastry. Decorate with slices of almonds if you wish.

Nusskämme (nut combs)

For 12 pieces of pastry:
½ recipe puff pastry, page 111
2 large baking sheets — Rinse sheets with water but do not dry.

Karottentorte (Carrot Torte)

Apfel Strudel (Apple Strudel)

Stollen

FILLING

1 cup medium-ground filberts	Mix all ingredients together.
⅓ cup sugar	
1 egg white	
2 tablespoons rum	

On a floured working surface, roll out puff pastry dough to a three-sixteenths-inch-thick rectangle, 20 inches long and 15 inches wide. Cut out twelve 5-inch squares with a pastry wheel or knife. Set on prepared baking sheets. Spread about 2 heaping teaspoons of filling lengthwise down the middle of each square. Brush one side of dough with beaten egg. Fold other half of dough over the filling, so that the edges of the dough are even. With a pastry wheel, make a number of comblike cuts three-quarters-inch apart, from the edge up to the filling. Chill for 30 minutes.

Preheat oven to 450°F. Before baking, brush with beaten egg. Place on the middle rack of the oven for 15 minutes, then turn the heat down to 400°F and bake for another 5 to 10 minutes, or until pastry has nicely browned.

If you wish, brush with sugar glaze as in apricot windmills.

Zungen (tongues)

Served as "double" tongues, with flavored whipped cream spread between them, they taste heavenly.

For 14 pieces of pastry, making 7 tongues:	
½ recipe puff pastry, page 111	
2 large baking sheets	Rinse the sheets with water, but do not dry.

Construct an oval-shaped pattern out of paper, 8 inches long and 2½ to 3 inches wide.

Roll out the dough to one-eighth-inch-thick on granulated sugar (instead of flour). Sprinkle more sugar on top. Place the paper pattern over the dough and cut out with a pastry wheel or knife, trying to place it so that dough scraps are kept to a minimum. Remove the cut-out dough to a prepared baking sheet. Prick the dough with a fork at one-quarter-inch intervals. Chill for 30 minutes.

Preheat oven to 450°F. Before baking, brush each pastry with beaten egg. Place in the oven at the middle level for 8 to 10 minutes, or until the pastry looks lightly browned. Watch carefully, however, since it burns easily because of the sugar. Prick the pastry several times more while baking if it rises too high.

Immediately unmold tongues onto a cake rack to cool. Serve on the same day, or freeze.

½ pint whipping cream, flavored with vanilla or liqueur

Whip cream until stiff. Spread about 2 tablespoons of cream onto one piece of pastry. Cover with a second. Dust top lightly with confectioners sugar.

Serve soon after the pastry has been filled.

Schweinsöhrchen (palmiers)

In Germany these little palm-leaf pastries are called "little pigs ears." But by any name, they taste as sweet!

For about 3 dozen palm leaves:
½ recipe puff pastry, page 111
2 large baking sheets   Rinse sheets with water but do not dry.

Roll out the dough on granulated sugar instead of flour. It should measure about 12 x 14 inches, one-eighth to one-quarter-inch-thick. Sprinkle with more sugar. Mark a center line down the length of the dough. Roll each half of the dough up to the center line, starting at the outside edge. The result resembles a scroll, a double roll of puff pastry connected on one side by a layer of dough. Chill for half an hour.

Remove from refrigerator and, holding the double roll tightly on its side, use a sharp knife to cut one-quarter-inch slices. Place each on a baking sheet about 1½ inches apart and open the design a little so they can expand in the oven. Chill again for 30 minutes before baking.

Place on the middle rack of a 425°F preheated oven for 8 to 10 minutes, or until palm leaves are caramelized on the bottom. Reset heat to 375°F, and turn pastries upside down with a spatula. Continue baking for another 3 minutes or so, until the other side is caramelized.

Loosen the palm leaves immediately when out of the oven and place separately on a rack to cool.

Hefeteig

(Yeast Dough)

Sweet yeast pastry is an important part of German baking. This classic dough is composed of simple ingredients; still, it needs some care in preparation so that it will produce a light, finely textured piece of pastry.

In the days when eggs, butter, and sugar had to be used in the most economical ways, sweet yeast pastry was a great treat for Sunday afternoon coffee. Since that time yeast goods have retained their popularity, and for a festive occasion a *Gugelhopf* has as honored a place on the table as the finest *Torte*.

Particularly in home baking, yeast dough often serves as a pastry shell for tarts, taking the place of the "richer" rich tart pastry dough. These tarts remind one of Grandma's delicate baking, of wedding parties in the countryside or *Kirchweihen* (harvest celebrations). They can be baked round, or as rectangular sheets called *Plattenkuchen* or *Blechkuchen* (sheet tarts and cakes).

Yeast pastry, with a few exceptions, is at its best when served the same day it is baked, or the next day. It freezes very well and can be thawed in an oven which has been preheated to 400°F and then turned off.

Preparing the Dough

Yeast dough only thrives when living conditions are favorable for the yeast organisms. A cozy, warm kitchen which is draft-free and perhaps a bit humid is the best starting place for a yeast dough. But cold temperatures are not the only thing yeast dislikes: heat above 140°F. is deadly for this one-celled plant. This is why all ingredients and utensils should be at room temperature and the added liquid always warm, but never hot. Mix salt, softened butter, and eggs with the flour, and not with the yeast mixture, since these tend to inhibit the yeast organisms from multiplying. The richness of the dough in terms of the amount of butter, eggs, sugar, nuts, and raisins used determines how much yeast is needed to make the dough light and porous; thus a simple dough needs only half the yeast of a rich *Stollen*.

The rising time of yeast dough depends on how warm your kitchen is. At 70° to 75°F it will rise a bit slower than at the perfect temperature of 80°F.

There are a number of ways to prepare the yeast for a dough. I prefer to make a yeast sponge variously called *Dämpfle, Hefel,* or *Vorteig,* depending on the geographic area of Germany. In prestarting yeast the cells are given a chance to multiply; this means less subsequent rising time for the dough. It is also a chance to see if the yeast is working as it ought to.

All recipes ask for unbleached all-purpose flour because of the higher gluten content. You may, however, substitute the bleached variety.

It is difficult to know beforehand the exact amount of liquid required for the dough. Be sure, therefore, to check the description of the dough you are making and use it as a guide.

For mixing ingredients and beating the dough, I like the traditional utensil, a wooden spoon with a hole in the middle, if no heavy-duty mixer is available.

About Yeast. The fresh, compressed yeast which I prefer is available in most markets, sold in 0.6-ounce cakes. The moist, living cells are pressed together with a small amount of starch as a binder. Fresh, compressed yeast is perishable and should be kept in a cool place. When buying it, check the date on the package to be sure it is still good. Fresh yeast is creamy white in color (not brown); it should be moist and should crumble easily. Stale yeast becomes slimy and gives off a strong odor.

Dry yeast keeps well for several months. It is dried in fine granular form and packaged in an airtight metal foil. One envelope of dry yeast equals one 0.6-ounce cake of fresh yeast.

Fresh or dry yeast can be dissolved in the same way.

Making Yeast Dough

By Hand

Make sure all ingredients and utensils (including the bowl) are at room temperature. Measure flour into the bowl and make a well in the center.

The yeast sponge is prepared as follows for all the recipes:

Dissolve the yeast (fresh or granulated) with half of the lukewarm milk plus 1 teaspoon sugar. If the recipe only calls for a few tablespoons of milk, use it all for the sponge. Pour into the flour well. With a fork, combine dissolved yeast with some flour to the consistency of pudding. Cover the bowl with a towel and place in a warm spot for 10 to 15 minutes. The mixture will rise slightly and look spongy and bubbly.

Cut the soft butter into slices and place around the flour mound. With a wooden spoon, mix more flour into the risen yeast mixture. Then add eggs, egg yolks, sugar, salt, flavorings, and the rest of the milk. Beat dough with the spoon against the sides of the bowl, incorporating all ingredients. At this point, check the description given in your selected recipe for the consistency of the dough. If the dough becomes too heavy to beat with the spoon, take it out on a lightly floured surface and knead with the palms of your hands anywhere from 7 to 15 minutes (depending on the amount of dough and the desired consistency). When the dough is first kneaded by hand, it may suddenly become somewhat thinner because of the soft butter which is now being worked into the dough. At this point, do not make the mistake of adding more flour; continue kneading for at least 5 minutes and then judge if more flour is needed. The finished kneaded dough may still feel sticky, but it should loosen itself from hands, bowl, or working surface, feel soft, and show blisters. If there are any additions such as raisins, nuts, or candied peel, add these now and knead into the dough just long enough to evenly distribute them. The dough will develop a muddy color if these ingredients are added too early in the process.

Place the dough into the bowl and cover with a towel. Unless otherwise indicated in the recipe, let it rise to double its volume so that the dough feels light and springy when pressed.

After the dough has risen, deflate it, take it out of the bowl, and knead lightly and briefly to remove the air bubbles.

Shape and let rise again according to your individual recipe.

By Heavy-Duty Mixer

Follow the preparations given in the hand method. Use a dough hook and turn the machine to the lowest setting. Combine yeast sponge with flour, then add all other ingredients. Increase the speed slightly, mixing for about 8 minutes. The dough should no longer stick to the side of the bowl. It should feel soft and look blistery. Now add other ingredients such as raisins, etc., and mix into the dough with only a few turns to distribute them evenly.

Continue as described in the hand method.

Baking Sweet Yeast Dough

A fairly hot, preheated 400°F oven is best for yeast baking. It insures that the outside crust of the pastry will be formed at the right time. If the oven is too hot, the result will be a dark crust with a doughy interior. With too low an oven heat, the baking gases disappear faster than the pastry rises, producing a heavy pastry.

Sometimes, sweet bread baked on baking sheets gets too brown on the bottom. This can happen if the oven heat comes only from the bottom. A second sheet under the baking sheet may help to solve the problem.

Unmolding

When using a mold, let cool for 5 to 10 minutes. Then unmold onto a cake rack so that air can circulate around the pastry, in order to avoid a soggy crust. Pastry baked on a sheet can be taken off immediately and unmolded onto a wire rack.

Hefeteigboden für Obstkuchen (yeast dough shell for tarts)

Tart shells made from rich pastry usually need prebaking before receiving fruit and filling. This is not necessary when making a tart shell from yeast dough. See the section on tarts, pages 38-61, and use filling recipes designed for unbaked or partially baked tart shells. All of them, except *Linzertorte,* may be enjoyed with a yeast dough base.

The *Kuchen* will be best if served on the same (or the next) day as baked.

Preheat oven to 400°F.
10-inch springform pan Butter the pan.

YEAST SPONGE

2 cups unbleached flour For making yeast dough, see pages 122-123
0.6 ounce (or 1 envelope, if dry) yeast
1 teaspoon sugar
⅓ cup milk

DOUGH

5 tablespoons unsalted butter, softened The dough should loosen itself from hands and working surface, but still feel rather soft.
3 tablespoons sugar
pinch of salt
1 egg
grated peel of ½ lemon

Let the dough rise to one-third more than its initial volume (about 1 hour at 75°F). Deflate the risen dough and knead again briefly. On a lightly floured surface, roll out the dough to a circle. Use your pan as a guide, making the circle large enough to fill out pan bottom and sides. Roll dough over rolling pin and place into pan. With your fingers, pat into place.

Fill with your selected filling and topping. Immediately bake on the lowest rack of a preheated 400°F oven for 30 to 45 minutes, depending on the filling. If you are using a soufflé-type filling, the baking time will be 40 to 45 minutes. Should the top brown too fast, place a piece of aluminum foil lightly over the tart to prevent burning.

Cool the tart for 10 minutes in the pan. Unbuckle the sides of the pan and wait another 10 minutes before unmolding it onto a wire rack. (See unmolding tarts, page 37.)

Hefeboden für Plattenkuchen
(yeast dough base for sheet tarts and cakes)

This yeast dough base can be used for any of the following sheet cakes. All are baked in a jelly roll pan, not on a baking sheet, so that fruit juices or bubbly fillings are kept in the pan. These cakes and tarts are best when served the same day as baked.

16 x 11 x 1-inch jelly roll pan   Butter the pan.

YEAST SPONGE

2 cups unbleached flour
0.6 ounce (or 1 envelope, if dry) yeast
1 teaspoon sugar
½ cup milk

For making yeast dough, see pages 122-123

DOUGH

3 tablespoons unsalted butter, softened
3 tablespoons sugar
pinch of salt
1 egg
grated peel of ½ lemon

The dough should loosen itself from hands and working surface but still feel rather soft.

Let the dough rise to one-third more than its initial volume (about 1 hour at 75°F). Deflate and knead again briefly. On a lightly floured surface, roll out the dough to fit the pan. Roll dough around rolling pin and place into pan. Continue with your chosen filling or fruit: see the following recipes.

Zwetschgendatsche (prune plum sheet tart)

Yeast dough base for sheet tarts, p. 125
2½ pounds firm prune plums   Cut the plums into halves.

Arrange the plums in rows, laying skin side down, overlapping slightly. Let dough rise for another 20 minutes before baking. Preheat oven to 400°F.

½ cup slivered almonds (optional)   Spread almonds on the plums.

Bake in the lower middle of a 400°F oven for about 30 minutes.

2-3 tablespoons sugar
½ teaspoon cinnamon

Mix sugar and cinnamon and spread over the hot cake. Cool and slice into rectangles.

Apfeldatsche (apple sheet tart)

Yeast dough base for sheet tarts, page 125
2 pounds crisp, tart, medium-sized apples
1 tablespoon lemon juice
1 tablespoon sugar
1 teaspoon cinnamon (optional)

On how to prepare apples, see page 9, but cut them into eighths. Toss apples with lemon juice and sugar.

Hefeteig 125

Arrange rows of apple slices so that they overlap slightly, leaving a one-quarter-inch border all around. Let the dough rise for another 20 minutes before baking it. Preheat oven to 400°F.

½ cup raisins
1 tablespoon sugar
½ cup medium-ground filberts, walnuts, or sliced almonds

Place raisins between apple slices. Spread sugar and nuts over the whole.

Bake in the lower middle of a 400°F oven for 30 to 35 minutes.

1 tablespoon sugar

When out of oven, dust again with sugar. Cool the cake and slice into rectangles.

Streusel Schnitten (crumb sheet cake)

Yeast dough base for sheet cakes, page 125
Streusel (double the recipe), page 147

Spread the streusel evenly over the dough. Let the dough rise for 20 minutes before baking it. Preheat oven to 400°F.

Bake in the lower middle of the oven for 20 to 25 minutes, or until the crumbs are golden brown.

Cool in the pan and when cold, slice into rectangles.

Bienenstich Schnitten (beehive slices)

Yeast dough base for sheet cakes, page 125
Bienenstich topping (double the recipe), page 25

Spread the topping evenly over the dough. Let the dough rise for 15 minutes before baking it. Preheat oven to 400°F.

Place a sheet of aluminum foil under the pan in case the topping bubbles over the pan sides. Bake in the lower middle of a 400°F oven for 20 to 25 minutes, or until the topping is golden brown.

Cool in the pan and when cold, slice into rectangles.

Gugelhopf

There are as many charming stories surrounding this sweet bread as there are spellings for its name. A *Gugel* was the long, conical headdress worn by ladies in the Middle Ages. With a little imagination it is not hard to connect this with the conical central tube of the *Gugelhopf* mold.

The dough is soft and sticky. More like a batter, it fills out the mold nicely. Butter, sugar, and eggs are beaten separately until fluffy and then mixed with the flour and yeast sponge.

9-10 inch *Gugelhopf* mold — Butter the mold heavily. Dust with flour or finely ground almonds.

YEAST SPONGE

4 cups unbleached flour
.6 ounces (or 1 envelope, if dry) yeast
1 teaspoon sugar
⅔ cup whole milk

Prepare yeast sponge with all the milk as described on page 122 and let rise for 10 to 15 minutes. In the meantime, prepare the beaten mixture.

DOUGH

¾ cup (1½ sticks) unsalted butter, softened
⅔ cup sugar
3 eggs
2 egg yolks
3 tablespoons whipping cream
grated peel of 1 lemon

With a wire whip or electric beater, cream the butter. Add slowly sugar, eggs, egg yolks, cream, and lemon peel. The mixture should look light and fluffy.

Add the mixture to the flour and yeast sponge. With a wooden spoon or in a heavy-duty mixer, combine all ingredients. Beat against sides of bowl until the dough is smooth and looks satiny.

1 cup raisins, plumped in boiling water for one or two minutes.

Drain and dry the raisins. Add to the dough and combine just enough to evenly distribute them.

Pour the dough into the prepared mold and cover with a towel. Allow to rise to double its volume (1 to 1½ hours at 75°F), or about one-half-inch from top of *Gugelhopf* mold.

Preheat oven to 400°F. Bake on the lowest rack for 45 to 50 minutes, or until a cake tester inserted comes out clean. Unmold onto a cake rack after 5 minutes of cooling.

Dust generously with confectioners sugar.

Gugelhopf is best when served one day after it has been baked.

Variation. You may, for a change, add the following to the dough mixture:

½ cup raisins, plumped
¼ cup diced candied lemon peel page 173-174
¼ cup diced candied orange peel, page 173-174
½ cup blanched, medium-ground almonds

Stir in with a few strokes just before dough is placed into mold.

Hefeteig

Hefekranz (yeast crown)

Braided yeast dough is baked not only in Germany but all over eastern Europe. In Swabia and elsewhere the braid is arranged in a circular shape to create a *Hefekranz,* or yeast crown. On Easter, the crown is filled with colorful eggs and served at breakfast.

14 x 16-inch baking sheet	Butter the sheet.

YEAST SPONGE

4 cups unbleached flour	For making yeast dough, see pages 122-123
0.9 ounce (or 1½ envelopes, if dry) yeast	
1 teaspoon sugar	
1 cup milk	

DOUGH

½ cup (1 stick) unsalted butter, softened	The dough should be soft but loosen itself from hands and working surface. Still, it ought to be thick enough to be shaped.
⅓ cup sugar	
2 eggs	
1 egg yolk	
grated peel of 1 lemon	
1-2 teaspoons anise seeds	
¾ cup raisins, plumped in boiling water for one or two minutes	Drain and dry the raisins.

When dough has risen to double its volume (about 1½ hours at 75°F), deflate it and knead again briefly. Slice the dough into three equal parts. With your hands, roll each piece to a 20-22 inch long roll. Place next to each other and braid the dough. If you have made a bigger recipe for a bigger crown, start with braiding in the middle to avoid stretching the dough. Place the braid on the prepared baking sheet and arrange as a circle.

Preheat oven to 400°F.

1 egg yolk	Brush the dough with egg yolk. Sprinkle on the sugar. Spread almonds on top.
several tablespoons crystallized sugar	
¼ cup slivered almonds	

The dough should rise only a short time, about 10 minutes, so that the top surface will crack open a bit during baking.

Place in preheated oven on lower middle rack for 25 to 30 minutes, or until a cake tester comes out clean. Unmold onto a wire rack to cool.

Wickelkuchen (rolled cake)

A filling with roasted filberts is spread on the rolled-out dough, which is baked in a loaf pan and then glazed.

loaf pan, 13 x 5 x 3½ inches or slightly larger. Butter and flour the pan.

YEAST SPONGE

4 cups unbleached flour
0.9 ounce (or 1½ envelopes, if dry) yeast
1 teaspoon sugar
1 cup milk

For making yeast dough, see pages 122-123.

DOUGH

½ cup (1 stick) unsalted butter, softened
⅓ cup sugar
pinch of salt
2 eggs
grated peel of ½ lemon

The dough should leave hands and working surface clean but feel rather soft.

While the dough rises to double its volume (about 1½ hours at 75°F) prepare the filling.

FILLING

3 cups finely ground filberts

Place ground filberts on a baking sheet and roast in a preheated 375°F oven for 15 minutes or until evenly brown. Cool the nuts before mixing with the egg whites.

2 egg whites
½ teaspoon vanilla extract
½ cup confectioners sugar

Mix together with the nuts. The filling will be rather thick.

Deflate the risen dough and knead again briefly. On a lightly floured surface, roll out the dough to a rectangle 13 inches long and 10 inches wide (adjust to fit the length of the pan). Spread the filling over the dough, leaving a 1-inch border all around.

½ egg white Brush egg white around border.

Roll up the dough lengthwise to make a 13-inch long roll. Combine both ends and seam with your fingers. Lift into prepared pan, seam down. Cover with a towel and let the dough rise for 15 to 20 minutes. Preheat oven to 400°F.

1 egg yolk Before baking, brush top of dough with beaten egg yolk.

With a sharp knife, make a one-quarter-inch deep incision lengthwise on top of dough. Bake in a 400°F oven on the lowest rack for 35 to 40 minutes, or until a cake tester inserted in the middle comes out clean. Unmold onto a wire rack.

Several tablespoons apricot preserves, page 166 Brush on top of hot pastry.

Optional:
White sugar icing, page 163, flavored with rum Spread over the hot glaze.

Hefeteig

Schwäbischer Kranz (Swabian crown)

The traditional filling for this crown is a little less rich than the more modern version given here. Under "variation" you will find the proper amounts for an old-fashioned Swabian Crown.

14 x 16-inch baking sheet — Butter the sheet.

YEAST SPONGE

4 cups unbleached flour
0.9 ounces (or 1½ envelopes, if dry) yeast
1 teaspoon sugar
¾ cup milk

For making yeast dough, see pages 122-123

DOUGH

6 tablespoons unsalted butter, softened
⅓ cup sugar
pinch of salt
2 eggs
grated peel of ½ lemon

This dough is fairly heavy and dry, but should still feel soft. While the dough rises to double its volume (about 1½ hours at 75°F) prepare the filling.

FILLING

1½ cups diced figs
2 ounces (½ cup) diced semisweet chocolate
½ cup blanched almonds, chopped.
½ cup sultanas, plumped in boiling water for one or two minutes.
¼ cup sugar

Mix all ingredients with the sugar. Set aside.

Deflate the risen dough and knead briefly. On a lightly floured surface, roll out the dough to a rectangle about 27 inches long and 10 inches wide.

3 tablespoons unsalted butter, melted — Brush the rolled-out dough generously with butter.

Evenly spread the filling over the dough. Roll up the filled dough along its length, making a tight 27-inch-long roll. With a sharp knife, cut the roll into two pieces with a single slash down its length. Turn the open sides upwards, so that the filling does not fall out. Starting in the middle, twist the two pieces together so they form a rope, with the filling still facing upwards. Move to the prepared baking sheet and combine the ends to form a circle. Place filling back where it may have fallen out. Cover with a towel and let rise for 15 minutes.

Preheat oven to 400°F. Bake on the lower middle rack for about 30 minutes, or until a cake tester comes out clean. Unmold onto a wire rack.

Simple sugar icing, page 164, flavored with rum — Spread over the hot pastry.

VARIATION FOR THE FILLING

¾ cup blanched almonds, chopped
¾ cup sultanas, plumped
¼ cup sugar
1 teaspoon cinnamon

Mandelstange (almond twist)

A superb coffee bread with a rich almond filling.

large baking sheet	Butter the sheet.

YEAST SPONGE

4 cups unbleached flour	For making yeast dough, see pages 122-123
0.9 ounce (or 1½ envelopes, if dry) yeast	
1 teaspoon sugar	
1 cup milk	

DOUGH

6 tablespoons unsalted butter, softened	The dough will be heavy and dry, but should still feel soft to the touch.
¼ cup sugar	While the dough rises to double its volume
2 eggs	(about 1½ hours at 75°F)
grated peel of ½ lemon	prepare the filling

FILLING

7 ounces (about 1½ cups) blanched almonds, finely ground	Mix ingredients to spreading consistency.
7 ounces (about 1½ cups) unblanched almonds, medium-ground	
3 egg whites	
¾ cup sugar	
½ teaspoon almond extract	
1-2 tablespoons rum.	

Deflate the risen dough and knead again briefly. On a lightly floured surface, roll out the dough to about 20 inches long and 30 inches wide. Spread the filling evenly over the dough. Roll up the dough to a 20-inch-long roll. With sharp knife, cut the roll in two parts lengthwise. Turn the open sides with the filling facing upwards. Twist the two parts together like a rope with the filling still facing upwards. Move to a prepared baking sheet and arrange the twist into a horseshoe shape or leave it straight, depending on how large your baking sheet is. Cover with a towel and let rise for 15 to 20 minutes. Preheat oven to 425°F. Bake on the lowest rack for 10 minutes. Then turn down oven heat to 400°F and bake for another 15 to 20 minutes, or until golden brown. Unmold onto a wire rack.

½ cup apricot preserves   Brush the glaze over the hot pastry.
    page 166
Optional:
1 cup simple sugar icing,   Spread icing over glaze.
    page 164, flavored with
    lemon juice or rum

Früchtebrot (fruitbread)

Also called *Schnitzbrot* or *Hutzelbrot*, it is rather different from the fruitcake you probably know. It is a simple yeast dough, loaded with dried fruits and nuts; the slices are served spread with unsalted butter. Tightly wrapped, it can be kept for several weeks. This recipe makes three loaves.

2 or 3 baking sheets   Butter the sheets.

PREPARING THE FRUITS AND NUTS

2 cups dried prunes   Place water, prunes, and pears in a saucepan
2 cups dried pears   and boil for a few minutes until fruit is
3 cups water   soft. Save the broth for the dough. Pit the
    prunes if necessary. Dice prunes and pears
    and place in a big bowl where you will add
    the other fruits, nuts, and spices.

2 cups raisins, plumped or
    soaked overnight in rum
2 cups (about 1 pound)
    figs, diced
2 cups walnuts, diced
½ cup candied lemon peel,
    page 173, diced
½ cup candied orange peel,
    page 173, diced
2 teaspoons anise seeds
1 tablespoon cinnamon
1 teaspoon ground cloves

DOUGH

8 cups unbleached flour   For making yeast dough, see pages 122-123.
3 ounces (or 5 envelopes,   Use ½ of the prune water in place of milk
    if dry) yeast   for making yeast sponge.
1 teaspoon sugar (for the
    yeast sponge)
2¼ cups reserved prune water
½ cup sugar

    Add the rest of liquid and the one-half cup sugar to the risen yeast sponge and flour and mix. The mixture may not look moist enough; this is all right, since more liquid can be added depending on the moisture content of the fruit. Place dough on a working surface. Start kneading the flour mixture together with the fruits, nuts, and spices. The dough should be very heavy but will still feel sticky (it will stick somewhat to your fingers and working surface). If you need to, add a little more liquid or flour. Place the thoroughly kneaded dough into a large bowl or onto a baking sheet and cover lightly with a towel. Situate in a warm spot, and let it rise about one-third over its volume (2 to 3 hours at 75°F).

Deflate the dough and divide into three equal parts. Shape three loaves, each about 8 inches long. Set on prepared baking sheets, cover again, let rise for another hour or until loaves show increased volume.

Preheat oven to 400°F. Bake in the lower middle of the oven for 30 to 40 minutes, or until a cake tester shows no uncooked dough. Unmold onto a cake rack. If you have more prune water left, brush the loaves with it. Dust with confectioners sugar.

Stollen

The *Stollen* is probably central Europe's best known yeast recipe. Dusted with powdered sugar, it symbolizes the infant Jesus wrapped in swaddling clothes. Each region has its own recipes and names—*Klaben* or *Klöben*, *Sächsisches Brot*, *Striezel*, and *Schittchen*, to name a few. When the times were poor, *Stollen* was made with rough bread flour, water, and a few raisins; but when the years were rich, *Stollen* became more elaborate, with butter, spices, and sugar. It was a custom, still observed at the beginning of this century, to bake several *Stollen* and give them as gifts for Christmas. Bake a *Stollen* one or two weeks before Christmas—it will improve with age.

14 x 16-inch baking sheet	Butter the sheet.

YEAST SPONGE

4½ cups unbleached flour	For making yeast dough, see pages 122-123.
1.5 ounces (or 2½ envelopes, if dry) yeast	
1 teaspoon sugar	
¾ cup milk	

DOUGH

1 cup (2 sticks) unsalted butter, softened	The dough should be heavy and should loosen itself from hands and working surface, but will feel soft because of the large amount of butter.
½ cup sugar	
2 eggs	
½ cup raisins	Plump raisins and sultanas or soak them in rum overnight.
½ cup sultanas	
¾ cup candied lemon peel page 173, diced	Knead in raisins, nuts, and peels at the very last.
¾ cup candied orange peel page 173, diced	
¾ cup blanched, finely diced almonds	

Hefeteig

Let the dough rise to double its volume (1½ to 2 hours at 75°F). Deflate and roll into an oval about 11 x 14 inches. The middle of the oval should be slightly thinner than the sides. Now fold the oval so that the bottom flap extends still about 1½ inches beyond the top flap. This will give you the traditional *Stollen* look. Cover with a towel and let rise on the baking sheet for 15 to 20 minutes.

Preheat oven to 400°F.

6 tablespoons unsalted butter, melted	Brush the dough with 1 tablespoon butter. Reserve the rest.

Bake on the lowest rack of the oven for about 45 minutes, or until a cake tester inserted comes out clean. Unmold onto a wire rack.

Brush the *Stollen* with the remaining 5 tablespoons of the melted butter, and while still hot, dust generously with confectioners sugar.

Wrap the cold *Stollen* in plastic and keep in a cool place.

Mohnstollen (Poppyseed *Stollen*)

Here is a *Stollen* richly filled with ground poppyseeds. After baking, it is glazed with lemon-flavored fondant.

14 x 16-inch baking sheet	Butter the sheet.

YEAST SPONGE

4 cups unbleached flour	For making yeast dough, see pages 122-123.
0.9 ounce (or 1½ envelopes, if dry) yeast	
1 teaspoon sugar	
¾ cup milk	

DOUGH

¾ cup (1½ sticks) unsalted butter, softened	The dough will be heavy. While the dough is rising to double its volume (about 1½ hours at 75°F), prepare the filling.
¼ cup sugar	
pinch of salt	
2 eggs	
grated peel of 1 lemon	
½ cup medium-ground almonds	

FILLING

¾ cup milk	In a heavy-bottomed saucepan, heat up the milk. Add butter and sugar to the hot milk. Turn off heat, add poppyseeds, lemon peel, and cinnamon. Mix well. Let this mixture stand for 30 minutes for the poppyseeds to swell.
3 tablespoons unsalted butter	
⅓ cup sugar	
2½ cups ground poppyseeds (slightly less than ½ pound)	
½ teaspoon cinnamon	
grated peel of ½ lemon	
1 egg	Before using, whip in the egg.

Deflate the risen dough. On a lightly floured surface, roll out the dough to a rectangle, 10½ inches wide and 16 inches long. Evenly spread the filling onto the dough, leaving a 1-inch border all around. Roll up the long sides of the rectangle tightly to meet at the center like a scroll. With your fingers, combine the ends and seam of the double roll. Move to the prepared baking sheet. Cover the *Stollen* and let rise for 20 minutes.

Preheat oven to 400°F. Bake on the lowest rack of the oven for 40 minutes, or until a cake tester comes out clean. Unmold onto a wire rack.

2 cups fondant, page 161 flavored with 2 tablespoons lemon juice	Pour the fondant over the Stollen.
¼ cup almond slices Or ¼ cup pistachios, chopped	Sprinkle nuts over the fondant.

Quarkstollen

Quark makes this *Stollen* very tender and moist.

14 x 16-inch baking sheet	Butter the sheet.

YEAST SPONGE

4½ cups unbleached flour 1.2 ounces (or 2 envelopes, if dry) yeast 1 teaspoon sugar ¼ cup milk	For making yeast dough, see pages 122-123

DOUGH

¾ cup (1½ sticks) unsalted butter, softened ¾ cup sugar 2 egg yolks 1½ cups *Quark,* pages 149-151 pinch of salt grated peel of 1 lemon	With a wire whip or electric beater, cream the butter. Add slowly sugar, egg yolks, lemon peel, and *Quark*.

Add the *Quark* mixture to the risen yeast sponge. Knead the dough until smooth. The dough will feel soft because of the *Quark*. But it should loosen itself from hands and surface and be heavy, otherwise the loaf will flatten out during baking.

1 cup raisins, plumped for 1 or 2 minutes in boiling water, or soaked in rum overnight	Knead the raisins into the dough.

Hefeteig

Let the dough rise to double its volume (1½ to 2 hours at 75°F). Deflate it and roll into an oval about 11 x 14 inches. The middle of the oval should be slightly thinner than the sides. Now fold the oval so that the bottom flap extends still about 1½ inches beyond the top flap. This will give you the traditional *Stollen* look.

Move the *Stollen* to the prepared baking sheet. Cover it with a towel and let rise for about 15 minutes.

Preheat oven to 400°F. Bake in the oven on the lowest rack for 45 minutes, or until a cake tester inserted comes out clean. Unmold onto a wire rack.

4 tablespoons unsalted butter, melted Confectioners sugar	Brush with butter, while still hot, then dust generously with confectioners sugar.

Plunderteig (Danish pastry)

Created in Vienna by a Danish pastry cook, this pastry has become an international favorite. A simple yeast dough is made tender and flaky as thin layers of butter are rolled into it.

If you are making Danish pastry for the first time, read the extensive introduction for puff pastry. The methods for preparing and rolling the butter into the dough are only slightly different. Danish pastry should be served the same day as baked. Or you may freeze it and later thaw the pastry in a 400°F preheated oven which has been turned off. Add glazes, icings, or confectioners sugar after defrosting.

YEAST SPONGE

4 cups unbleached flour 0.9 ounce (or 1½ envelopes, if dry) yeast 1 teaspoon sugar 1 cup milk	For making yeast dough, see pages 122-123.

DOUGH

5 tablespoons unsalted butter ¼ cup sugar pinch of salt 2 eggs grated peel of 1 lemon (optional)	Knead dough until smooth for about 5 minutes by hand. (The dough does not need to be elastic.) It should loosen itself from hands and working surface, but still feel rather soft.

When dough is kneaded into a smooth ball, dust with flour, wrap in wax paper, and place into refrigerator for 20 minutes. In the meantime, prepare the butterbrick.

1 cup (2 sticks) unsalted butter, chilled but pliable 2 tablespoons flour	On wax paper, form the butter into a 6-inch-square brick. Coat each side with 1 tablespoon flour. Chill again if necessary. The shaped butter should have the same consistency as the dough so they can be rolled out together successfully.

Flour the working surface and rolling pin and roll out the dough to a rectangle 22 inches long and 8 inches wide.

Cut butterbrick into two equal parts. Place one part into the middle of the rolled out dough and fold bottom part of dough over it. Place second butterbrick on top and fold the top part of the dough over it. With your fingers, combine the seams.

Turn the dough package a quarter turn counterclockwise so that the top flap is on your right, facing you like a book.

Again, roll the dough into a rectangle 20 x 8 inches in size. Then fold again in three even parts like a letter, as previously done. You have now completed the first turn. Dust the dough with flour, wrap in wax paper, seal in plastic, and chill for 20 minutes.

Repeat three more times the rolling and folding of the dough exactly as with turn one. Leave a rest period of 20 minutes between each turn. It is important that the dough have the top flap with its open side on the right every time the dough is rerolled.

After the fourth turn, chill the dough for 2 hours before rolling and shaping for the individual recipes.

Quarktaschen (cheese pockets)

2 large baking sheets Danish pastry, pages 136-137 For twelve 6-inch pastries	Butter the sheets.

FILLING

1 cup *Quark,* pages 149-151 1 egg yolk ¼ cup sugar ¼ teaspoon vanilla extract grated peel of ½ lemon	Beat *Quark* until smooth. Add egg yolk, sugar, and flavoring.
½ cup sultanas, plumped	Mix in sultanas.
1 egg white	Beat egg white separately and fold into the *Quark* mixture.

On a floured surface, roll out the dough to about one-eighth inch thick, 24 inches long, and 18 inches wide. With a pastry wheel or knife, divide into twelve 6-inch squares. In the middle of each square place 1½ tablespoons of filling. Fold each of the four corners up to the middle to enclose the filling

Hefeteig

completely. Pinch together the seams a bit. Place on to the prepared baking sheet. Cover the pastry with a towel and let rise for about 20 minutes, until the dough feels light and springy when touched. Preheat oven to 425°F.

1 egg yolk, beaten with 1 teaspoon water	Brush the surface with beaten egg.

Bake on the middle rack for 15 to 20 minutes, or until the pastry is nicely browned. Unmold onto a wire rack.

1½ cups apricot preserves, page 166	While pastry is still hot, brush with glaze. Dust generously with confectioners sugar.

Schneckennudeln (cinnamon snails)

2 large baking sheets Danish pastry, pages 136-137 For about 18 snails	Butter the sheets.

FILLING

1 cup raisins, plumped ½ cup medium-ground almonds ½ cup sugar 2 teaspoons cinnamon	Mix together and set aside.

On a floured surface, roll out the dough to a rectangle, about one-quarter-inch thick and 16 inches wide.

4 tablespoons unsalted butter, melted	Brush the dough with melted butter.

Spread the filling evenly over the dough. Roll it up tightly, making a 16-inch-wide roll. With a sharp knife, cut three-quarters-inch thick slices. Place on the prepared baking sheets. Cover with a towel and let rise for about 20 minutes, until the dough feels light and springy when touched. Preheat oven to 425°F.

1 egg yolk, beaten with 1 teaspoon water	Brush top of snails

Place in the oven on the middle rack for 15 to 20 minutes, or until the pastry looks nicely browned. Unmold onto a wire rack.

1½ cups fondant, page 161,
   flavored with rum or lemon
	Spread about 2 tablespoons of fondant on
	   each pastry.

Gefüllte Hörnchen (filled crescents)

2 large baking sheets ½ recipe Danish pastry, pages 136-137 For 12 crescents	Butter the sheets.

FILLING

1 cup finely ground toasted filberts
¼ cup sugar
1 egg white
¼ teaspoon cinnamon (optional)

Toast the ground nuts in a 375°F oven to an even brown. Let cool. Mix with egg white and sugar.

On a floured surface, roll out the dough to one-eighth-inch thick, 18 inches long, and 12 inches wide. With a knife or pastry wheel, cut six 6-inch squares. Cut each square in half along the diagonal. Spread 1 teaspoon filling in the middle of each triangle. Starting along the longest side, roll up the dough so that the point is on the outside. Set on the prepared baking sheet, bending each roll into a crescent. Cover with a towel and let rise for about 20 minutes, until the dough feels light and springy when touched. Preheat oven to 425°F.

1 egg yolk, beaten with
1 teaspoon water

Brush with egg.

Place in a 425°F oven for about 15 minutes, or until the pastry looks nicely browned. Unmold onto a wire rack.

1 cup apricot preserves, page 166

Brush hot pastry with glaze. Dust generously with confectioners sugar.

Hefeteig 139

Kleingebäck

(cookies)

Only once a year, at Christmas, do cookies really come into their own in Germany. Advent Sunday marks the time when traditional family recipes are retrieved from the bottoms of kitchen drawers and cookie baking starts.

The selection and variation of cookies from each region in Germany is enormous and to describe all of them would require a book in itself. Here are just a few to give a taste of these cookies which, after all, can be enjoyed not only at Christmas.

About Baking and Storing

When a cookie sheet is reused in baking, clean it off carefully and butter anew. Place cookies only on a cold baking sheet—otherwise they may lose their shape. Always allow ample space between them, as they tend to spread in baking. Cool cookies on a wire rack. They will keep for weeks when stored in an airtight container in a cool place.

Marillenringe (filled ring cookies)

When it is all put together, this *Mürbteig* (rich tart pastry) cookie looks like a tiny tartlet. A solid round cookie is covered by a ring cookie of equal size. It is filled with apricot preserves and dusted with confectioners sugar.

This recipe makes about 32 cookies.

DOUGH

2½ cups unbleached flour
¾ cup sugar
1 cup (2 sticks) unsalted butter
1 egg yolk
a pinch of salt
grated peel of ½ lemon

For how to make *Mürbteig* (rich tart pastry), see pages 34-35.

Press the dough into a ball, wrap in wax paper and then in plastic wrap, and refrigerate for at least three hours. (You may make the dough a few days ahead of time, as with any *Mürbteig*.)

Preheat oven to 375°F.
Several baking sheets   Butter the sheets lightly.
2½-inch or slightly larger cookie cutter, scalloped or plain
1 to 1¼-inch cookie cutter for cutting out the center of the rings

Cut the dough in two and refrigerate one half until needed. With your knuckles, knead the dough to a flat circle on a floured working surface. The dough has to stay cold—otherwise it will be impossible to roll out. With a lightly floured rolling pin, roll out the dough about one-eighth-inch thick. Cut out an even number of solid and ring cookies (about 32 of each). Place the same kind on one baking sheet so they will bake uniformly. Prick each cookie several times with a fork to prevent air pockets.

Bake at the middle level of a preheated 375°F oven for 8 to 10 minutes or until very pale golden in color. With a spatula, immediately take cookies off the baking sheet and place them on a wire rack to cool.

FILLING

¾ cup apricot preserves   If the preserves are cold, warm up to room temperature.

Spread a thin layer of preserves on the solid cookie. Place the ring on top. Dust generously with confectioners sugar. Then fill out the ring with more preserves.

Store the cookies in a cool place.

Variation. Cut only rings (no solid cookies). Before baking, sprinkle some crystallized sugar and coarsely chopped, blanched almonds on half of the rings, leaving an equal number plain. When they are baked, sandwich them together using some preserves as a filling.

Spitzbuben (little rascals)

This fine cookie dough is a *Mürbteig* (rich tart pastry) with almonds. Three different sizes of cookies are stacked on top of each other and held together with raspberry preserves. Finish with a light frosting or a dusting of confectioners sugar.

This recipe makes 25 cookies.

DOUGH

1½ cups unbleached flour
½ cup sugar
½ cup (1 stick) unsalted butter
¾ cup finely ground, blanched almonds
1 teaspoon vanilla extract

For how to make *Mürbteig* (rich tart pastry), see pages 34-35.

Note: Because there is no egg to bind the dough, it will take a little longer for it to form a ball. Repeatedly compress the dough in the palms of your hands and release it.

Press the dough into a ball, wrap in wax paper and then in plastic wrap, and refrigerate for at least two hours. (You may make the dough a few days ahead of time.)

Preheat oven to 375°F.
3 large baking sheets
3 round cookie cutters in graduated sizes, 1½-inch, 1¾-inch, 2-inch, or slightly larger. Scalloped edges look the nicest.

Butter the sheets.

Lightly flour the working surface and the rolling pin. In case you double the recipe, cut the dough in two and refrigerate one-half until needed. If the dough is very cold, let it warm up so that you can knead it to a flat circle on the working surface. The dough may crumble into a thousand pieces—but do not let this worry you. Just push the pieces together with your fingers, then take the rolling pin and roll over it. Repeat this until you are able to bind the dough together and roll it out to about one-eighth-inch thick. Do not let the dough get too warm—otherwise it will stick to the rolling pin, making it difficult to roll out the dough smoothly.

Cut out the same number of cookies in each of the different sizes (about 25 of each).

With a flat, unserrated knife, loosen the cookies from the working surface and place on the prepared baking sheet. Place the same size cookies together on one sheet so they bake evenly.

Bake in a 375°F preheated oven on the middle rack for 8 to 10 minutes or until they have a very pale golden color. Once out of the oven, immediately remove the cookies with a spatula onto a wire rack to cool.

FILLING

½ cup red raspberry preserves

If preserves are chilled, warm up to room temperature.

Spread a thin layer of preserves on the largest cookie. Cover with the second cookie. Spread the second cookie with preserves and place the small one on top.

Dust the assembled cookies lightly with confectioners sugar or cover with a thin frosting.

FROSTING

3 cups confectioners sugar
5 tablespoons lemon juice
2 tablespoons water

Make as in Simple Sugar icing, page 164.

Set cookies on a wire rack and pour over a very thin layer of frosting.

Teebrot (tea bread)

This is an old family recipe, and Christmas at our house could never be celebrated without these cookies. They taste richly chocolate with a touch of cinnamon. The traditional cookie cutter is 3 and one-half inches long and has an hourglass shape. But if you use any other shape cutter, it will taste just as good.

This recipe makes about 130 cookies, depending on the cookie cutter.

DOUGH

½ cup (1 stick) plus 2 tablespoons unsalted butter
1¼ cups sugar
2 eggs

Cream butter, sugar and eggs, using one of the methods on pages 11-13.

grated peel of ½ lemon
2 teaspoons ground cinnamon

Add lemon peel and cinnamon.

4 ounces unsweetened chocolate, finely ground
3 cups unbleached flour

Fold in chocolate and flour.

Shape this rather soft dough into a ball. Wrap in wax paper, slip in a plastic bag, and refrigerate for 24 hours.

Preheat oven to 400°F.
Several baking sheets
Any cookie cutter

Butter the sheets.

Slice the dough in two and refrigerate one-half of it until needed. Lightly flour the working surface and rolling pin. Keep the dough cold while rolling out to a three-sixteenths-inch thickness. Cut the dough in the desired shapes and place the cookies onto a prepared baking sheet, 1½ inches apart.

2 egg yolks
2 teaspoons cold milk

Beat egg yolk with milk and brush on the top of each cookie.

Bake on the middle level of a 400°F preheated oven for 8 to 10 minutes. With a spatula, place immediately on a wire rack to cool.

Vanillebrötchen (vanilla cookies)

The preparation of vanilla cookies is very simple. However, they need a drying period of at least 24 hours before they are baked. As a result of the drying, the bottom of the cookie forms a pedestal for the meringue-like top.

This recipe makes 35 to 40 cookies.

Two large baking sheets	Butter the sheets well.

BATTER

3 eggs, at room temperature 1 cup sugar 1½ teaspoons vanilla extract 2 cups sifted flour	Break eggs into a mixing bowl and start beating on medium (if you use a mixer) until they are foamy. Add the sugar by spoonfuls, and add the flavoring. Increase speed to medium-high and beat until the mixture is very thick and pale yellow in color. Change to a wire whip and gently fold in the flour.

With the help of another spoon, drop a heaping teaspoon of batter onto the prepared baking sheet. Leave about three inches between each cookie, since they will expand.

Place the sheets of unbaked cookies in a cool, dry place (not in the refrigerator) for at least 24 hours. When the surface of the cookies feels dry, they are ready for baking.

Bake in a preheated 350°F oven on the middle rack for 15 to 17 minutes. With a spatula, remove the cookies to a wire rack to cool.

Himbeerbrötchen (raspberry cookies)

These delicately flavored cookies are similar to the vanilla cookies. This recipe makes about 40 cookies.

2 large and 1 small baking sheets	Butter the sheets well.

BATTER

3 eggs, at room temperature 1 cup sugar 3 tablespoons raspberry preserves 2¼ cups sifted flour	See previous recipe, Vanillebrötchen (vanilla cookies), for instructions.

Haselnussmakronen (filbert meringue cookies)

White meringue and a whole filbert top this elegant drop cookie. The recipe makes about 30 cookies.

Preheat oven to 350°F.
Several baking sheets — Butter the sheets well.
30 whole filberts

BATTER

4 egg whites, at room temperature
1 cup sugar
juice of ½ lemon

Beat egg whites on low speed until foamy. Slowly increase speed and beat until they form soft peaks. Add the sugar by spoonfuls. Then add lemon juice all at once. Continue beating until the mixture is thick.
Reserve one cup of meringue in a separate bowl for the topping.

1 teaspoon vanilla extract
2½ cups finely ground filberts (about ½ pound)

With a wire whip, fold in the vanilla and all of the ground nuts.

Drop one tablespoon of batter with the help of a second spoon on the prepared baking sheet. Leave two inches between each cookie. With a teaspoon, place enough of the reserved meringue on the cookie to cover the top nicely. Position one whole filbert into the center of each.

Place on the middle level of a preheated 350°F oven for about 15 minutes or until the cookies are very lightly browned. Once out of the oven, wait about two minutes before taking them off the sheet. With a spatula, place the cookies on a wire rack to cool. The cookies will become firmer as they cool.

Wespennester (wasps' nests)

A light and tasty mouthful of nuts and chocolate, perfectly spiced. This drop cookie looks like what its name suggests.
This recipe makes 30 to 35 cookies.

Preheat oven to 350°F.
Several baking sheets — Butter the sheets well.
2 cups (7 ounces) unblanched almonds, slivered — Place slivered almonds on a baking sheet and toast in a 350°F oven for 5 minutes or until light brown. Set aside to cool.

BATTER

3 egg whites, at room temperature
¾ cup sugar
½ teaspoon vanilla extract
¼ teaspoon ground cinnamon
⅛ teaspoon ground cloves
3 ounces semisweet chocolate, finely ground
toasted almonds

Beat egg whites on low until foamy. Slowly increase speed and beat until soft peaks form. Add the sugar by spoonfuls. Then add vanilla, cinnamon, and cloves. Continue beating until the mixture is thick.

With a wire whip, gently fold in the chocolate and the nuts.

Drop one heaping teaspoon of batter with the help of a second spoon on the prepared baking sheet. Leave two inches between each cookie.

Bake in the middle of a 350°F preheated oven for 15 minutes. Immediately remove the cookies with a spatula to a wire rack to cool.

Toppings, Frostings, Fillings, and Decorative Candies

Streusel (crumb topping)

Streusel topping is encountered on many different kinds of German baked goods. Just as it is said that there are many ways to heaven, so there are many excellent recipes for streusel. I think very highly of this particular one—it is my grandmother's.

I prefer making streusel by hand, since it goes very rapidly. If you would rather use a heavy-duty mixer, pay careful attention that it does not become overmixed.

½ cup plus 2 tablespoons unsalted butter, chilled	Cut the butter into quarter-inch slices. Place all ingredients together in a large bowl. Working quickly with one hand so that the butter does not melt, squeeze the butter into the flour and sugar. Pick up handfuls and squeeze-release into the bowl. Continue to squeeze and release until all flour and sugar is incorporated into butter and the streusel is loose and crumbly.
⅔ cup sugar	
1¾ cups flour	
½ teaspoon vanilla extract	
1 teaspoon cinnamon	
Or	
grated peel of ½ lemon	

Adding the Streusel Layer. Hold a handful of streusel over the batter in the pan and break large pieces with your fingers into pea-sized lumps (this does not have to be exact; but make sure there are lumps and the streusel is not reduced to powder). Repeat until the topping is evenly distributed over the batter.

Quark

This is the essential ingredient for *Käsekuchen* (cheesecake). A German baker without at least one *Käsekuchen* in his repertoire is as unthinkable as a Polish pianist who can perform no Chopin. And all the many varieties of German cheesecake have one thing in common: they all begin with *Quark*.

Quark, which in earlier times was called *Milchkäse* (milk cheese) or *Weisser Käse* (white cheese), is an uncured cheese. Milk is allowed to stand at room temperature until it turns to *Sauermilch* (clabbered milk). This is heated in a water bath until thick. Then it is cooled and drained in a fine sieve.

In Germany you can buy *Quark* containing varying amounts of cream so that the cook can make adjustments according to what the recipe calls for. The classic *Käsekuchen* (also called *Quarkkuchen* in some parts of Germany) combines *Quark* with sweet or sour cream, eggs, and flavorings; the mixture is spread over *Mürbteig* (rich tart pastry) and baked to a beautiful golden brown. There are many other uses for *Quark*, and I have included a sampling of recipes to show what can be done with it. See the index for listings.

About Commercial Cheeses: Cottage, Pot, Farmer's, and Baker's. These cheeses, also unripened, would seem the natural substitute for *Quark* in American baking; perhaps you have seen German recipes calling for one of them. Indeed, the process for making *Quark* described above is the way cottage cheese is made "down on the farm."

However, the tangy taste and creamy texture which make *Quark* so special are completely missing in these commercial products. They are far too bland and have a lumpy, sometimes even grainy texture which makes for a rough, heavy cake batter. These are simply no substitute for German *Quark* or for the homemade product below.

How to Make *Quark*

After much trial and error, not to mention letters to Germany, I have produced a cheese using homogenized milk which looks and tastes like the German *Quark*. Fortunately, it is easy to make.

Note: The milk-buttermilk mixture must stand at room temperature for at least 24 hours, so plan to make *Quark* a couple of days before you need it. Finished *Quark* keeps up to five days under refrigeration.

The following recipe makes about 3 cups of *Quark*.

double boiler or heavy-bottomed saucepan	A tin-lined copper pot or any other heavy saucepan is imperative, since too much heat will result in grainy *Quark*.
glass, porcelain, or pottery bowl or jug	
2 quarts whole milk	Place milk and buttermilk into container and stir to blend. Cover and allow to stand undisturbed at room temperature for 1 to 2 days, until milk is thick. It will smell slightly sour.
1 cup cultured or churned buttermilk (must be without additives such as tapioca, etc., or it will not thicken properly)	

Using a Double Boiler. Pour the milk into a barely simmering double boiler. In a few minutes the milk will begin to shrink from the edges of the pan, and the surface will look somewhat solid. After 5 minutes in the water bath, insert a knife into the center of the *Quark*. If it comes out clean, it is done, but if milk still coats the blade of a knife, leave the *Quark* on the heat longer and test again in a few minutes. The liquid surrounding the *Quark* will also be clear when it is done. Take the pan out of the water bath and set aside to cool.

If your double boiler does not hold all of the milk, you may make the *Quark* in two batches. Place the first batch aside in a bowl to cool while you prepare the second. Do not drain the *Quark* while still hot.

Using a Heavy-Bottomed Saucepan. Place milk into the pan and turn heat to medium. Watch carefully for the moment when the milk begins to shrink from the sides of the pan. When this happens, turn heat immediately to the lowest possible setting. Using the knife test described above, test the *Quark* after about five minutes. When done, allow to cool in the pan.

When the *Quark* is completely cool, place it into a fine sieve to drain. Refrigerate, if it is not to be used immediately.

Note: The liquid (whey) which drains from the *Quark* should be clear, containing no visible milk solids. If it is cloudy, the *Quark* was not heated long enough and it should be returned to pan or double boiler. A yellowish color and graininess indicates that the *Quark* was heated too long. Whey, incidentally, can be saved and used in place of water in bread baking.

For about 2 cups of *Quark*:
1½ quarts whole milk
¾ cup buttermilk

For about 1 cup of *Quark*:
3 cups whole milk
6 tablespoons buttermilk

Buttercremes (buttercreams)

Egg yolks, sugar, butter, and flavoring, beaten together to a creamy mass, make what is called an *Echte* (real) buttercream. However, buttercreams may also have a custard base, which makes them lighter and less rich. This recipe makes about 2 cups.

BASIC BUTTERCREAM

1 cup (2 sticks) unsalted butter, softened
¾ cup confectioners sugar
2 egg yolks
2 tablespoons whipping cream (optional)

Beat butter, sugar, egg yolks, and cream at a moderate speed until the buttercream is smooth, light, and fluffy. Chill until cold but still spreadable. Then fill and frost cakes and tortes.

VANILLA BUTTERCREAM

basic recipe plus
1 tablespoon vanilla extract

COFFEE BUTTERCREAM

basic recipe plus
3 tablespoons very strong coffee

RUM BUTTERCREAM

basic recipe plus
3 tablespoons dark rum
Other flavors:
add 3 tablespoons cognac,
    orange liqueur, or kirsch
    to basic recipe.

CHOCOLATE BUTTERCREAM

basic recipe plus
1 teaspoon vanilla extract
3 ounces semisweet
    chocolate
½ ounce unsweetened
    chocolate

In a double boiler, melt chocolate over barely simmering water. Cool chocolate until it is warm. Add to fluffy buttercream and whisk until well combined. Chill until cold but still spreadable.

CHOCOLATE NUT BUTTERCREAM

basic chocolate buttercream
    plus
1 cup finely ground almonds,
    filberts, or walnuts

MOCHA BUTTERCREAM

basic chocolate buttercream,
    but omit vanilla extract and
    add 3 tablespoons very
    strong coffee

FILBERT BUTTERCREAM

basic recipe plus
2 teaspoons vanilla extract
1 cup finely ground filberts

ALMOND BUTTERCREAM

basic recipe plus
¼ teaspoon almond extract
1 cup finely ground,
    blanched almonds

KROKANT (TOASTED ALMOND BRITTLE) BUTTERCREAM

basic recipe plus
1 teaspoon vanilla extract
1 cup toasted almond brittle

PINK BUTTERCREAM

basic recipe plus
3 tablespoons puréed
    strawberries, raspberries,
    or cherries

Buttercreme mit Creme Unterlage
(buttercream with custard base)

I can't praise this superb cream enough. It is excellent for the filling of tortes or for an outstanding dessert with fruit. This recipe makes about two cups.

½ cup sugar
2 tablespoons cornstarch
¼ cup cold milk
¾ cup hot milk
4 egg yolks

Place sugar and cornstarch into an unheated double boiler. Add ¼ cup of cold milk and mix until well blended. Whisk in the egg yolks, one at a time. Pour in the hot milk very slowly, while vigorously beating the mixture. Turn heat to medium and beat the cream constantly until very thick. Remove from water bath and cool. Stir from time to time to prevent a skin from forming.
(Have custard at the same temperature as the butter.)

½ cup (1 stick) unsalted butter, softened
1-2 tablespoons kirsch, orange liqueur, rum, cognac, or other liqueur
Or
2 teaspoons vanilla extract
Or
½ cup finely ground nuts
Or
¾ cup finely grated chocolate
Or
2-3 tablespoons very strong coffee

Beat the butter until fluffy. Slowly add the custard and blend well with the butter.
Add flavoring and blend with the cream.
Chill the buttercream until it reaches spreading consistency.

Schokoladen-Buttercreme mit Creme Unterlage
(chocolate buttercream with custard base)

Here is a chocolate version of the custard-based buttercream. This recipe makes about 2 cups.

3 ounces semisweet chocolate
½ ounce unsweetened chocolate

Melt chocolate in a double boiler over low heat. Set aside to cool.

CUSTARD

¼ cup sugar
2 tablespoons cornstarch
¼ cup cold milk
¾ cup hot milk
2 egg yolks

Place sugar and cornstarch into an unheated double boiler. Add ¼ cup of cold milk and mix until well blended. Whisk in the egg yolks. Pour in the hot milk very slowly, while vigorously beating the mixture. Turn heat to medium and beat the cream constantly until very thick. Remove from water bath and stir until warm.

Add the melted chocolate and blend with the cream.

1 tablespoon vanilla extract

Whisk in the flavoring. Cool the cream to room temperature (same as the butter).

½ cup (1 stick) unsalted butter, softened

Beat the butter until fluffy. Slowly add the custard and blend well with the butter. Chill the buttercream until it reaches spreading consistency.

CHOCOLATE RUM BUTTERCREAM

basic recipe, but omit
    vanilla extract and add
2 tablespoons dark rum

MOCHA BUTTERCREAM

basic recipe plus
2-3 teaspoons powdered
    instant coffee

CHOCOLATE NUT BUTTERCREAM

basic recipe plus
½ cup finely ground walnuts,
    filberts, or almonds

Vanille Creme (vanilla cream)

This cream can be used as it is for the filling of tortes and cakes. If you wish, refine it with whipped cream.

For about 2 cups of cream:

½ cup cold milk
1½ cups hot milk
4 tablespoons cornstarch
½ cup sugar
6 egg yolks
1 tablespoon unsalted
    butter
2 teaspoons vanilla
    extract

Place cornstarch and sugar into an unheated double boiler. Add ½ cup of cold milk and mix until well blended. Whisk in the egg yolks, one yolk at a time. Pour in the hot milk very slowly, while beating the mixture vigorously. Add butter and flavoring. Now turn heat to medium and whisk the mixture constantly until the cream is very thick. Remove from water

Or
1-2 tablespoons rum, kirsch, cognac, or orange liqueur

bath and cool. Stir from time to time to prevent a skin from forming.

The following addition makes for 2¾ cups of cream:

½ pint whipping cream
2 tablespoons confectioners sugar

Whip cream with sugar until stiff.

With a wire whip or electric beater, beat vanilla cream until smooth. Gently fold in the whipped cream. Chill until it has thickened to spreading consistency.

Orangen (oder Zitrone) Buttercreme
(orange or lemon buttercream)

This excellent buttercream can be made either with oranges or lemons. This recipe makes about 2¼ cups, enough to fill one layer and frost a 9 or 10-inch cake.

ORANGE CREAM

½ cup (1 stick) unsalted butter
⅔ cup sugar
grated rind of 1 orange
⅓ cup orange juice, strained
1 tablespoon frozen, concentrated orange juice
5 egg yolks

In a heavy saucepan over low heat, melt the butter. Stir in the sugar with a wire whip. When well blended, add orange juice and rind. Add egg yolks one at a time, and beat until the mixture is thick and coats a spoon. Let cool until tepid.

LEMON CREAM

In place of oranges, use:

grated rind of 1 lemon
juice of 2 lemons

This is the basic cream which is now turned into a buttercream with the addition of more butter.

½ cup (1 stick) unsalted butter, softened
1 tablespoon orange liqueur
Note: Omit orange liqueur when making lemon buttercream, and add only the butter.

Beat butter with a wire whip or electric beater until light and fluffy. Add orange liqueur. Slowly add the orange cream and blend well. Be sure the cream is at the same temperature as the whipped butter, otherwise it will curdle. Chill to spreading consistency.

Toppings, Frostings, Fillings and Decorative Candies

Schokoladencreme mit Schlagsahne
(chocolate cream with whipped cream)

If you decide on something less rich than a buttercream, try this light chocolate cream. It is good for a filling or frosting, but it does not stand up very well in warm weather. This recipe makes about 3 cups, enough to fill one layer and frost a 9 or 10-inch cake.

4 ounces semisweet chocolate
½ ounce unsweetened chocolate (optional)
⅓ cup whole milk
2 tablespoons cornstarch
3 egg yolks
1 teaspoon vanilla extract
½ pint whipping cream
2 tablespoons confectioners sugar

In a double boiler over low heat, melt chocolate. Off heat, add milk and cornstarch and whisk briskly. Beat in one egg yolk at a time. When mixture is smooth, place over low heat again and beat until thick. (Do not allow to boil.) Off heat, add flavoring. Chill.

Whip cream with sugar until stiff. Fold whipped cream into the chilled chocolate cream. Refrigerate to spreading consistency.

RUM CHOCOLATE CREAM

basic recipe, omitting
    vanilla extract but adding
1 tablespoon dark rum

MOCHA CREAM

basic recipe plus
1-2 teaspoons instant coffee

Pariser Creme (Parisian cream)

I don't know of a more utterly delicious chocolate cream than Parisian cream. This cream, which is appreciated all over Europe, is excellent for filling and frosting.

Here are two recipes: the first includes only a moderate amount of chocolate, while the second is extra potent for chocolate addicts.

FOR ABOUT 2½ CUPS

1 pint whipping cream
8 ounces semisweet chocolate

Place cream and chocolate in a double boiler over low heat. Stir with a wire whip until chocolate has melted. Turn heat to high and stir the mixture until slightly thickened (about 3 to 5 minutes). Remove from water bath and stir to cool. Chill overnight or until cream has set.

Note: if you prefer an airier to a more velvety texture, whip the cream (just as you would whipped cream) until fluffy. It will not increase much in volume, but will become lighter. If necessary, refrigerate for a while so it again attains spreading consistency.

FOR ABOUT 3 CUPS

1 pint whipping cream
12 ounces semisweet chocolate
2-3 tablespoons confectioners sugar

Place cream, chocolate, and sugar in a double boiler. Proceed as above.

If you wish to whip the cream, it needs to be chilled only a couple of hours beforehand.

MOCHA CREAM

basic recipe plus
3 tablespoons instant coffee and additional confectioners sugar to taste

Schlagsahne (whipped cream)

In their love of *Schlagsahne* (whipped cream), the Germans are not far behind the Austrians. Whenever there is something sweet on the plate—be it cake, ice cream, or almost any other dessert—there is always some space for a dollop of whipped cream. A spoonful may also crown a cup of coffee or chocolate, not to mention iced coffee, where it is a *sine qua non*. In the home it appears in a bowl which is passed around the table so that everybody can help themselves.

Schlagsahne is always lightly sweetened and is sometimes flavored with liqueur. Used as a filling or frosting it will often include chocolate, nuts, candy, and any flavoring from rum to orange juice.

When whipping cream the same principle applies as with egg whites. The idea is to get as much air as possible into the cream so that it will double in volume. Whether you beat the cream with a wire whip or an electric mixer, start very slowly and gradually build up speed. All recipes in this book call for stiffly beaten whipped cream.

If the whipped cream is to be prepared as much as a day in advance, its keeping power will be enhanced by the addition of one-half teaspoon of dissolved gelatin for every cup of whipping cream. This procedure is explained.

FOR ABOUT 2 CUPS OF WHIPPED CREAM

½ pint (1 cup) whipping cream, also called heavy cream
2 tablespoons confectioners sugar, unless otherwise indicated by individual recipe

Whipping cream, bowl, and beater should be thoroughly chilled. Start to beat very slowly, circulating the beater all around the bowl until the cream begins to foam. Increase speed gradually to medium. When cream stands in soft peaks, add the sugar and flavoring. Beat with a few more turns until the cream stands in stiff peaks. Do not beat beyond this stage, otherwise it will become granular and finally turn into butter. Chill the cream until serving. It will keep a few hours in the refrigerator.

WHIPPED CREAM WITH GELATIN

½ pint whipping cream
2 tablespoons confectioners sugar
½ teaspoon powdered, unflavored gelatin
1-2 teaspoons water

In a small measuring cup, over low heat, dissolve gelatin with water. Cool until mixture is warm (gelatin must remain liquid). Beat the cream, using the above directions, until cream begins to stiffen. Continue beating and add slowly the dissolved gelatin. Add sugar and flavoring. Chill until using, up to 1 or 2 days.

FLAVORED WHIPPED CREAM

basic recipe plus
1-1½ tablespoons rum, cognac, orange liqueur, kirsch, or other liqueur
  Or
1-2 teaspoons vanilla extract
  Or
¼ teaspoon almond extract
  Or
1 tablespoon frozen, concentrated orange juice, thawed
  Or
2 tablespoons puréed fruit, such as strawberries, raspberries, or cherries

In case you are using sweet liqueur or fruit, you may use only 1 tablespoon confectioners sugar, or none at all depending on taste.

CHOCOLATE WHIPPED CREAM

basic recipe plus
1 teaspoon vanilla extract
2 ounces semisweet chocolate, finely ground

Toppings, Frostings, Fillings and Decorative Candies

COCOA WHIPPED CREAM

basic recipe plus
2 tablespoons confectioners
    sugar
3 tablespoons sifted cocoa

COFFEE WHIPPED CREAM

basic recipe plus
1 tablespoon confectioners
    sugar
1-2 teaspoons instant
    coffee (powdered)

ALMOND WHIPPED CREAM

basic recipe plus
¾ cup finely ground,
    blanched almonds
¼ teaspoon almond extract

FILBERT WHIPPED CREAM

basic recipe plus
¾ cup finely ground
    filberts
1 teaspoon vanilla extract
    Or
1 tablespoon rum

WALNUT WHIPPED CREAM

basic recipe plus
¾ cup finely ground
    walnuts
1 tablespoon dark rum

COCONUT WHIPPED CREAM

basic recipe plus
¾ cup dry, unsweetened
    coconut
1 tablespoon confectioners
    sugar

KROKANT WHIPPED CREAM

basic recipe plus
¾ cup *Krokant* (toasted
    almond brittle)

NOUGAT WHIPPED CREAM

basic recipe plus
1 cup finely ground
    nougat

Cremes für Obstkuchen (custard fillings for tarts)

The following two custards, simple to make, are particularly well-suited for filling fruit tarts. They are thick enough to support the weight of fruit and can be cut into serving pieces. You may also serve them chilled—plain or with fruit—for a dessert. In that case they can be made fancier by adding butter, whipped cream, or beaten egg whites.

Molding the Custard. These fillings cannot be poured warm into the tart shell without soaking the crust, and once they have thickened, they cannot be spooned into the shell without being completely broken up. But there is an easy solution to this problem: chill the custard in a well-buttered 9-inch mold, such as a round cake layer pan or springform pan. Unmold it whole into a 10-inch tart shell where it will make a snug fit.

Unmolding the Custard. Run a knife around the edge of the custard. Turn the pan upside down and unmold directly into the tart shell. It should unmold easily—if not, dip the pan into warm water for a few seconds and try again.

Note: The gelatin custard will be very thin until it is chilled, so make certain your mold will hold liquid without leaking. If not, partially chill the custard in the saucepan (about 1 to 1½ hours) until it thickens slightly. Then pour it into the molding dish until it is firm, which will take about 2 to 3 hours longer.

Creme mit Stärkemehl (cornstarch custard)

For about 2½ cups:

5 egg yolks ¾ cup sugar	Beat egg yolks and sugar together in a bowl with a wire whip or electric beater until the mixture turns pale yellow and thickens.
½ cup sifted cornstarch 2 cups whole milk 2 tablespoons unsalted butter	Add cornstarch and mix well. Pour the milk into a heavy-bottomed saucepan. Add the butter and the egg-sugar mixture to the milk, blending well with a wire whip. Bring to a boil over medium-high heat, stirring constantly. The custard will begin to thicken in lumps, but will smooth out as you continue beating. Turn down heat, but let the custard simmer for about 3 minutes more to cook the cornstarch. *Stir constantly.*

2 teaspoons vanilla extract
  Or
1 vanilla bean
  Or
	Remove from heat and add one of the suggested flavorings. Mold the custard as previously described.

160   Toppings, Frostings, Fillings and Decorative Candies

2 tablespoons dark rum,
   kirsch, cognac, or
   orange liqueur
   Or
½ cup finely ground, blanched
   almonds with ¼ teaspoon
   almond extract
   Or
½ cup finely ground
   filberts with 1 teaspoon
   vanilla extract
   Or
grated peel of 1 lemon
   with 1 teaspoon vanilla
   extract

Note: This custard can be kept up to 5 days under refrigeration, or it may be frozen.

Creme mit Gelatin (gelatin custard)

For about 2½ cups:

3 egg yolks	Beat egg yolks and sugar together in a bowl with a wire whip or electric beater until the mixture turns pale yellow and thickens.
¾ cup sugar	
2½ cups whole milk	Pour the milk into a heavy-bottomed saucepan. Add the gelatin to the cold milk. Place over low heat, stirring constantly, until gelatin is completely dissolved. Remove from heat when the milk almost reaches the boiling point. Beat in the egg-sugar mixture.
1½ envelopes (1½ tablespoons) unflavored, powdered gelatin	
choice of flavorings: see previous recipe for cornstarch custard	Add one of the suggested flavorings. Mold the custard as previously described.

Note: Gelatin custard can be kept up to 3 days under refrigeration. Do not freeze.

Schmelzender Zuckerguss (fondant frosting)

There is much to be said for fondant, this loveliest of sugary *accessoires*; it has a beautiful velvety sheen and a fine texture and taste. And it is actually fun to make!

Preparing fondant is not at all difficult, if you pay attention to each step. Sugar syrup is boiled to the soft ball stage, cooled until it is tepid, and then kneaded with a spatula until it goes from clear to snowy white.

You can always keep a jar of fondant in the refrigerator, ready for frosting, since it keeps indefinitely. It can be reheated a few times, though it will lose some of its sheen in the process. This recipe makes about 4 cups, enough frosting for a 10-inch cake (top and sides) with some left over.

A marble surface, a large metal tray, or a jelly roll pan (no teflon)	Prepare the pan before you start cooking the syrup. Rinse tray or pan with water, leaving a few drops.
4-quart, heavy-bottomed saucepan	Dissolve cream of tartar in water in the saucepan, then add sugar. Turn heat to medium. Swirl pan slowly until the liquid comes to a boil and clears. Do not stir with a spoon. Cover the pan and raise heat to high: this will steam down sugar crystals left on the side of the pan. (There must be no crystallized sugar in the fondant.) Leave covered for a few minutes until syrup begins to thicken. Uncover and continue boiling until a candy thermometer indicates a temperature of 238°–240°F, the "soft ball" stage. If you do not have a candy thermometer, drop a bit of the syrup in cold water as a test; if it makes a "soft ball" when pressed lightly between the fingers, it is at the right consistency.
1½ cups water	
½ teaspoon cream of tartar	
4½ cups sugar	

Immediately pour the syrup into the prepared pan or onto the marble. Let it cool about 10 minutes until it is tepid and wrinkles on the surface when touched. With a sturdy metal spatula or turner, knead the syrup vigorously for 5 to 10 minutes, spreading the mass and pushing it together, until the syrup begins to cloud. If you have some leftover fondant you wish to add to the batch, now is the time to do it: it will help speed the crystallizing process. As the fondant turns snowy white and becomes impossible to knead any longer, scrape it together in a ball at the center of your working area. The whole process may take a bit longer than 10 minutes, so don't become discouraged if the fondant fails to whiten on time.

Store in an air-tight container in the refrigerator, or let ripen overnight to develop its fullest bloom.

How to use fondant: set the cake on a rack placed over a tray to collect any frosting which runs down.

4 cups fondant (approximately)	In a double boiler, over simmering water, combine fondant and flavoring. Stir as fondant softens. It will be a smooth, glossy cream and should coat the spoon.
2-3 tablespoons rum, kirsch, orange liqueur lemon juice, or strong coffee	

Or
1½ teaspoon vanilla extract plus
1-1½ tablespoons water
Several drops of food coloring, if you wish

Note: If overheated it will lose its shine and creaminess. If too thick to be spread, thin with a little plain corn syrup.

FOR CHOCOLATE FONDANT

8 ounces semisweet chocolate, melted
3-4 tablespoons water

Mix melted chocolate with the melted fondant. Use 3 or 4 tablespoons water, depending on thickness of the fondant.

Immediately pour fondant over the cake, which has been brushed with hot apricot glaze (see page 166). Let it run down over the sides. If your cake is slightly concave on top and the fondant tends to puddle, move it quickly out of the center with a knife or spatula; it will set very rapidly. If you plan to embed decorations in the top of the cake, do so immediately before the fondant completely hardens. You may ice petits fours or candy by dipping them into fondant.

Weisser Zuckerguss (white sugar icing)

This type of frosting can be prepared very quickly. It is thick enough to use for writing or for decorative dribbles over pastry. However, confectioners sugar contains a small amount of cornstarch, and because this is an unboiled icing, you may be able to taste the starch. If this will bother you, better to try a cooked icing. This recipe makes about 1 cup of icing.

2 cups confectioners sugar
1 egg white
2 tablespoons lemon juice, rum, kirsch, orange liqueur, strong coffee, or fruit juice
Or
2 tablespoons orange juice plus
1 tablespoon frozen concentrated orange juice

Place sugar and flavoring in double boiler. Combine with a wire whip over simmering water. Add egg white and whisk the mixture until very fluffy and thick (about 10 minutes). Remove from water bath and beat until icing reaches spreading consistency. Pour evenly over the cake. This icing sets very fast. If you wish, place into a warm oven for a moment to give the icing more sheen. Let dry before slicing the cake.
If you wish the icing to be very thick for writing with a pastry bag or paper cornucopia, use only 1 tablespoon flavoring.

Toppings, Frostings, Fillings and Decorative Candies

Einfache Zuckerglasuren (simple sugar icings)

The following icings, like white sugar icing, are made from confectioners sugar. They are simple to make and easy to spread. This recipe makes about 2 cups.

PUNCH ZUCKERGUSS (PUNCH ICING)

5 cups confectioners sugar
3 tablespoons lemon juice
2-3 tablespoons dark rum
3 tablespoons raspberry
    juice or syrup

Place all ingredients in a double boiler over simmering water. Stir until icing has warmed and looks smooth and shiny. The icing should coat the back of a spoon fairly well to be right for spreading. If it is too thin, either wait a while until it has thickened, or add more confectioners sugar. In case the icing is too thick, add either more flavoring or water.

RUM ZUCKERGUSS (RUM ICING)

5 cups confectioners sugar
5-6 tablespoons dark rum
2 tablespoons water

KAFFEE ZUCKERGUSS (COFFEE ICING)

5 cups confectioners sugar
7-8 tablespoons very strong
    coffee

ZITRONE ZUCKERGUSS (LEMON ICING)

5 cups confectioners sugar
7-8 tablespoons lemon juice,
    strained

ORANGEN ZUCKERGUSS (ORANGE ICING)

5 cups confectioners sugar
7-8 tablespoons orange
    juice
    Or
6-7 tablespoons orange
    juice, plus
1 tablespoon frozen, concentrated orange juice

Gekochter Schokoladen-Zuckerguss (chocolate sugar frosting)

This crisp, sugary frosting is related to fondant. It needs a little more care in preparation than other icings, but if you follow directions exactly you will have no trouble. A candy thermometer here is a great help. This recipe makes about 1½ cups, enough for a 9 or 10-inch cake.

4 ounces semisweet chocolate
1 ounce unsweetened chocolate
1 cup sugar
¾ cup water
1 teaspoon vanilla extract
1 tablespoon unsalted butter

Melt chocolate in a double boiler over barely simmering water. Add sugar, water, and vanilla and combine with chocolate. Remove from water bath and place directly over a medium high flame. Cook the mixture, constantly stirring, for about 10 to 15 minutes, or until it reaches 220°F on a candy thermometer or spins a fine thread when dripped from a spoon. (The mixture will have slightly thickened.) Off heat, beat in the butter. Beat the frosting against the sides of the pan until it is tepid, smooth, and thick, but still pourable. Then pour over the cake which is set on a cake rack and spread evenly with a spatula. The icing will need several hours to set completely.

Schokoladen-Butterglasur (chocolate butter frosting)

In this simple icing, softened butter is beaten into melted chocolate. It can be used to make a very thin coating over cakes and tortes. This recipe makes about 1 cup, or a thin coating for a 9 or 10-inch cake.

4 ounces semisweet chocolate
½ ounce unsweetened chocolate
½ cup (1 stick) unsalted butter
1 teaspoon vanilla extract
   Or
1 tablespoon rum or cognac
   Or
¼ teaspoon almond extract

In a double boiler, over barely simmering water, melt the chocolate. Turn off heat and whisk in butter. When smooth, add flavoring. Chill to spreading consistency.

Schokoladenglasur mit Eiweiss (chocolate frosting with egg white)

Here is a frosting with a taste reminiscent of fudge. It is especially nice for small pastries or cakes belonging to the *Rührkuchen* family. This recipe makes about 1¼ cups, enough for a 9 or 10-inch cake.

Toppings, Frostings, Fillings and Decorative Candies

1½ cups confectioners sugar 1 egg white 3 tablespoons cocoa 1 teaspoon vanilla extract 2 teaspoons hot water 6 tablespoons unsalted butter, melted	Blend sugar, egg white, cocoa, water, and vanilla in a double boiler. Turn heat on low and let the mixture get warm but not hot. Constantly stir until smooth. Off heat, add the butter slowly, leaving the milky residue behind, and whisk briskly. Chill to spreading consistency. Stir frosting from time to time.

Marmeladeglasur (apricot preserves glaze)

A thin coating of apricot preserves is necessary under sugar frosting to seal the cake so that the frosting will not be absorbed. This gives the cake a smooth surface and adds more "gloss" to the final frosting. This recipe makes about 1 cup, enough to glaze a 9 or 10-inch torte.

1 cup apricot preserves	Stir preserves over low heat until melted. Rub through a fine sieve to leave the bits of skin behind. If not immediately used, place in refrigerator where it will keep for several months.

If a torte is to be filled with preserves, you may wish to give the preserves some additional flavor.

1 cup apricot (or other) preserves 1 tablespoon rum, kirsch, cognac, or orange liqueur	Proceed as above, adding flavoring last. If you prefer, leave bits of fruit in the preserves. While glaze is still hot, coat the cake with a thin layer, using a pastry brush. Allow to dry before the torte is frosted.

Geleegüsse (glazes)

Glazes add a wonderful final touch to cakes, tarts, or tortes, making them glisten.

Here are two. One is made with currant, peach, plum, cherry, or apple jelly which is boiled down to between 225° and 228°F. These jellies contain enough natural pectin to be sufficiently stiff for glazing at this temperature. The other glaze is a clear gelatin topping. This one is especially nice in the summer over fresh fruit tarts and fruit tortes. Whereas the first glaze is quite sweet, the second preserves fruit and gives it a beautiful, cool shine without adding very much sweetness. The one trick to using gelatin is to keep a very close watch on it and to pour it over the cake, tart, or torte just before it completely gels.

Johannisbeer Geleeguss (red currant glaze)

For about 1½ cups glaze, enough for a 10-inch cake:

1½ cups red currant jelly (or cherry, plum, peach, or apple jelly)
2 tablespoons sugar
1-2 tablespoons rum, kirsch, or other liqueur

In a heavy-bottomed saucepan, combine jelly, sugar, and liqueur. Boil until the glaze coats a spoon lightly and the last drops to fall from the spoon are sticky and hold their shape. A candy thermometer will show 225° to 228°F. Use the glaze immediately while still hot. Glaze may be cooled and warmed later to spreading consistency.

If there is no jelly available, use preserves or jam in the following way. Stir the preserves over heat until melted. Then rub through a sieve to remove the bits of skin. Proceed as with jelly.

Gelatin Geleeguss (gelatin glaze)

For about 1½ cups glaze, enough for a 10-inch cake:

1 envelope (1 tablespoon) powdered, unflavored gelatin
1½ cups water
¼ cup sugar
1-2 tablespoons rum, kirsch, cognac, or orange liqueur (if you use sweet liqueur, use less sugar)

Place all ingredients in a saucepan. Over low heat, stir until gelatin is dissolved (do not boil). Place into the refrigerator to chill. Keep a close watch on the gelatin and as soon as it starts to gel, spoon over the torte or tart. If you have missed that moment, place again over low heat and liquefy just enough to enable you to spoon it over the surface of your cake.

Konfekt (candies and chocolates)

I have only included a few of these sweet mouthfuls from the limitless variety available. They make nice decoration for tortes, and they certainly make good eating by themselves. German housewives often purchase ready-made chocolates from the selection of the local *Konditorei*. If you have a favorite "store bought" chocolate that you think might go well with a torte, do not hesitate to use it for decoration.

What Americans would call "chocolates," Germans call in general *Pralinen* (Pralines). This word, used in English only to describe nut-sugar candies, derives from the seventeenth century French nobleman, Marshall du Plessy-Pralin, whose cook was the first to brown almonds in boiling sugar.

All of the sweets in this chapter can be made long in advance and kept in the refrigerator or freezer. Rum balls need a few days to ripen to their best flavor.

Rumkugeln (rum balls)

Makes about 35 rum balls, three-quarters to 1 inch in diameter

6 ounces semisweet chocolate
4 tablespoons unsalted butter, softened
1 cup spongecake crumbs, ground very fine
¼ cup raisins, finely sliced
2-3 tablespoons dark rum
½ cup cocoa
  Or
½ cup confectioners sugar

Melt chocolate in a double boiler over low heat. Beat in the softened butter. Add crumbs, raisins, and finally the rum. Stir vigorously until well combined. Chill until firm enough to shape into little balls.

Take the mixture out with a teaspoon and place into the cocoa or sugar. Coat the balls by rolling them in the powder. Refrigerate until firm. When firm, you may wish to roll them in cocoa or sugar again.

Trüffel Pralinen (chocolate pralines)

Makes about 38 pralines 1 inch in diameter, 1½ inches long

1 cup marzipan (almond paste), page 171
1 cup powdered nougat, page 171
⅔ cup medium-ground, blanched almonds, lightly roasted
up to ⅓ cup whipping cream
piece of wax paper buttered

Combine with almond paste, nougat, and almonds just enough whipping cream to form a very thick paste.

Fill one teaspoon with the mixture and with the help of a second spoon, drop pralines on the wax paper. Give them an oval shape. Refrigerate or freeze until firm.

2 ounces unsweetened chocolate
½ cup (1 stick) unsalted butter, softened

In a double boiler, over low heat, melt chocolate. Swirl in the butter and blend well.

With a fork, dip the pralines into the chocolate to give them a thin coating. You may coat them completely or coat only the top. Place on a platter and allow them to set.

Orangenkugeln (orange balls)

Makes about 26 orange balls, three-quarters to one inch in diameter

168   Toppings, Frostings, Fillings and Decorative Candies

1¼ cups finely ground, blanched almonds
½ cup thick orange marmalade, (bitter or sweet)
1 teaspoon orange liqueur
½ cup dry, unsweetened coconut shreds

Add liquer and about ¼ of the marmalade to the ground nuts. Sitr. It should be a thick paste. If too thick, add more marmalade. (You may need up to ½ cup).

Shape little balls and coat with coconut.

Nougatkugeln (nougat balls)

For about 35 *Nougatkugeln,* three-quarter-inch in diameter

4 ounces semisweet chocolate
1 cup confectioners sugar
about ¼ cup strong coffee
1½ tablespoons cocoa
2 teaspoons vanilla extract
1 cup finely ground filberts
Or
1 cup finely ground almonds, unblanched
1 cup medium-ground semisweet chocolate
Or
use imported truffel chocolate, ground medium fine

Melt chocolate in double boiler over low heat, Take out of water bath. Add sugar, cocoa, and vanilla. Mix with a wire whisk, and add 2 tablespoons coffee. Add the nuts and, if necessary, some more coffee (you may need up to ¼ cup). The mixture should be fairly thick. Let cool until you can handle the mixture. Shape little balls, about ½ or ¾ inch in diameter.

Coat the balls with chocolate. Chill until firm.

Schokoladentrüffel (chocolate truffles)

For about 32 balls, three-quarter-inch in diameter

4 tablespoons unsalted butter, softened
1 cup confectioners sugar
1 teaspoon powdered instant coffee
¼ cup cocoa
2 tablespoons dark rum
½ cup cocoa

Cream butter with half of the sugar. Add coffee, cocoa, rum, and rest of sugar. Beat until the mixture is light and fluffy. Chill until you can shape a ball.

Take mixture out with a teaspoon and drop into cocoa. Roll it in cocoa, shaping a ball.

Toppings, Frostings, Fillings and Decorative Candies

Mandelsplitter (almond splinters)

For about 25 *Mandelsplitter* 1 inch in diameter, 1½ inches long

2 tablespoons unsalted butter ¼ cup cocoa ¾ cup confectioners sugar 1 tablespoon hot water 2 tablespoons orange liqueur Or 2 tablespoons kirsch 1¼ cups slivered, blanched almonds	In a heavy-bottomed saucepan over low heat, melt the butter. Add the sugar, cocoa, and hot water. Mix vigorously and add the flavoring. Stir in almonds.
large piece of wax paper, generously buttered	Fill one teaspoon with the mixture, and with the help of a second spoon, drop the *Mandelsplitter* on the wax paper. Give them an oval shape. Chill until firm.

Krokant (toasted almond brittle)

Krokant is a favorite *Konfekt* (candy) of Germany, rivaling marzipan (almond paste) in popularity. At Easter time, colorfully decorated *Krokant* eggs filled with chocolates are sold in *Konditoreien* throughout the country.

Krokant is used extensively for decorations on tortes and cakes (see *Frankfurter Kranz,* page 80) or is used in fillings. Wherever it is used, it also adds its own fine flavor.

For about 1½ cups:

10-inch heavy-bottomed skillet 4 tablespoons unsalted butter ½ cup sugar	Heat butter and sugar together over low heat, stirring constantly, until the sugar is dissolved.
1 cup medium-fine ground, blanched almonds	Increase heat to medium and add the almonds. Continue stirring until the nuts are browned lightly and evenly.

Note: If the nuts are cooked too long or over too high heat they will become dry, dark, and bitter.

Spread the *Krokant* on buttered foil or a wooden board to cool. Then crumble the cooled *Krokant* with your fingers or a potato masher, or put a handful at a time into an electric blender for a few seconds, to break it into small pieces, about the same size as oatmeal flakes.

Krokant freezes perfectly for several months in an airtight container.

Nougat

Nougat is similar to *Krokant*, but is made without the addition of butter. *Krokant* is always made with almonds alone; nougat usually with half almonds and half filberts. However, you may prepare pure almond or pure filbert nougat.

well-buttered surface such as a Formica top or marble slab
buttered knife
buttered cookie cutters (if you want to make decorations)
1½ cups sugar
1 tablespoon lemon juice
1½ cups medium-ground blanched almonds
1½ cups medium-ground filberts
Or
3 cups almonds
Or
3 cups filberts

For decorative pieces:

For nougat powder:

Place sugar in a heavy-bottomed skillet, preferably an iron pan, and cook over low heat until light yellow. Add lemon juice and nuts and continue to stir with a wooden spoon or metal spatula until it is a deep golden color. Pour out on the buttered surface. With the buttered knife, spread evenly.

Immediately cut your chosen shapes with a knife or cookie cutter. You have to work fast, since the nougat hardens very quickly.

Let nougat cool. Break into small pieces. Pulverize in a blender or nut grinder. Store in an air-tight jar.

Nougat keeps in the freezer for many months.

Marzipan (almond paste)

It is the Arabs to whom we owe the introduction of almonds into European cooking. Almonds were used in ancient Persia and first came to southern Europe during Roman times. Folk etymology would even have it that the word "marzipan" derives from one of the Roman emperors whose legions brought it back from the East: "Panis Marcius," bread of the Emperor Marcius. Reality is more prosaic; "marzipan" is probably just a corruption of an Arabic term.

Almonds appeared in northern Europe as trade routes opened during the late Middle Ages. Marzipan was first made and sold by apothecaries as *Kraftbrot* (power bread), and was reputed to cure insomnia, tuberculosis, and other assorted ills. Its medical virtues aside, sweetened almond paste has remained a very popular treat in Europe until the present day. As staples, Americans continue to prefer the walnut and the peanut, both excellent and substantial foods, but for delicacy and subtlety of flavor, I think there is no match for the noble Arabian almond.

Though it is an ingredient in some cakes such as *Margaretenkuchen* (see index), marzipan is most often used as frosting and for decoration. Frequently it is colored and shaped into miniature flowers, vegetables, or fruits. Little cherries, pears, strawberries, bananas, and apples, for example, are formed in their characteristic shapes complete with green leaves and stems. When one sees such an assortment stacked in a woven marzipan basket, one surely has to admire the artistry of the *Konditor* who creates such a delight for eye and palate. It cannot be eaten without regret!

In times past, the towns of Lübeck and Königsberg rivaled each other in the production of marzipan. Lübecker marzipan is still characterized by its slight "bitter" almond flavor, whereas the Königsberger is flavored with a few drops of rose water, suggesting the Orient.

The German housewife can buy marzipan ready-made, but I have not found a satisfactory almond paste on the American market, so I have started making it myself. Not only is this better, it is much cheaper as well. All one needs is a blender or a nut grinder to pulverize the almonds; the method is very simple.

Preparing Marzipan

Ordinarily a blender is undesirable for grinding nuts because they give up their oil and do not produce a loose powder. However, this is perfectly all right for preparing almond paste. German marzipan is made with a combination of sweet and bitter almonds. Since one cannot buy the strongly aromatic bitter almonds in the United States, it is necessary to include a small amount of almond extract in the recipe to strengthen the flavor.

For about 1 cup marzipan:
1 cup whole blanched almonds, pulverized with a blender
1 cup confectioners sugar
2 tablespoons cold water
¼ teaspoon almond extract
For Königsberger marzipan: reduce the almond extract to
2 drops and add
3 drops rose water

Place ingredients (and several drops food color, if desired) together in a heavy-bottomed saucepan. Turn heat on low and stir vigorously with a wooden spoon. *Note:* Watch heat carefully. If it is too hot the almond paste will darken and taste roasted. Stir until almond paste shrinks from the pan sides and bottom (about 3 minutes) and forms a ball around the spoon. It is now a thick paste. Take out of pan and place on a smooth surface. Let it cool enough so it can be handled, but don't let it get cold. Knead several times. The marzipan can be shaped immediately, or it can be used as it is for a cake batter.

For marzipan decorations: Use a Formica top or marble slab as a working area. Dust the working area lightly with confectioners sugar. Roll out the almond paste in the desired thickness. Cut out figures with a cookie cutter or sculpture them by hand.

Almond paste can be kept indefinitely in the freezer when tightly wrapped in wax paper and sealed in plastic. It keeps very well in the refrigerator, but will dry out slightly if it is stored too long.

Geraspelte Schokolade (shaved chocolate)

As a very effective decoration, use on top of a torte or brush on the sides.

Have the chocolate at room temperature. Take about 2 rows from a bar of semisweet or unsweetened chocolate in one hand and a vegetable peeler in the other. With even, slow motion, shave the chocolate. Allow the shavings to drop on a plate. This will give you a nice variety of big and small shavings.

When decorating a torte, pick the chocolate shavings up with a spatula and place directly on top or sides of the torte.

Orangeat und Zitronat (candied orange and lemon peel)

Making it yourself will insure you the finest quality candied orange or lemon peel. It is very tasty eaten just like candy, but it is mostly used in baking—added to the batter or utilized as decoration.

Three large oranges or 4-5 lemons give about one-half-pound or 3 cups of candied peel. Use fruit with a thick skin which has not been artificially colored.

Peel oranges or lemons (including the pith), making four or six pieces. Place in a glass jar and cover with water. Let stand in the refrigerator for three or four days, changing the water twice a day (and adding a few drops of lemon juice each time to prevent discoloration if you are soaking orange peel; this is unnecessary with lemon peel).

The reason for soaking the peel is to remove the bitter flavor. Taste before proceeding with the next step. If the peel is still bitter, allow it to stand for another day.

Drain the peel into a colander. Cut into julienne strips or whatever shape you desire. Place in a saucepan, along with a few drops of lemon juice, a big pinch of salt, and sufficient water to cover. Simmer for 1 to 2 hours, or until the peels are soft. (The amount of time required depends on how tender the peel is.)

When the peel is soft, drain very well in a colander. Weigh the peel. Combine with an equal weight of sugar and 1 to 2 tablespoons water in a heavy-bottomed saucepan. I have found that 3 cups of peel equals about 1 cup of sugar. Bring to a boil and continue stirring over high heat until the water has boiled out and sugar covers the peel. Be very careful not to caramelize the sugar.

Place the now-candied peel on a platter and allow to cool until it is warm. As soon as you can handle it, coat each piece with confectioners sugar or fine granulated sugar. Place on a rack to dry.

Store in the refrigerator in an air-tight glass jar. It will keep for several weeks.

Glossary

Gugelhopf (Turk's Head) mold—a fluted pan with a central tube.
Kirschwasser (Kirsch)—a clear cherry brandy. Real *Schwarzwälder Kirschwasser* comes from the Black Forest region of Germany and is made from black, sweet cherries. There is no alcohol, sugar, or flavor added in the fermentation process.
Kleinbäckerei—small pastries and cookies.
Konditorei—a German pastry shop.
Konfekt—candy, confectionary.
Krokant—toasted almond brittle; a candy made from almonds, sugar, and butter.
Marzipan—almond paste; made from pulverized almonds and sugar which are worked into a paste.
Mürbteig—rich tart pastry; this cookie-like dough serves as the crust or shell for tarts and tartlets.
Plattenkuchen—sheet tarts; made with yeast dough.
Pralinen—chocolate candies.
Quark—an uncured cheese; similar to cottage cheese, used in baking for cheesecakes and fillings.
Rehrücken (Saddle of Venison) mold—a ribbed pan about 12 inches long, used for a chocolate nut loaf.
Sandkuchen—a pound or butter cake.
Schlagsahne—whipped cream.
Stollen—a rich sweet yeast bread, served at Christmas.
Streusel—crumb topping for cakes and pastries.
Tart—flat, usually open-faced, fruit-filled pastry shell; related to the American pie.
Tartlet—small tart baked in a little mold.
Torte—a filled and decorated layer cake.

Sources of Baking Equipment and Supplies

Baking equipment and supplies are available from the following companies. Each has a mail-order catalogue.

Kitchen Glamor Inc.
26770 Grand River,
Detroit, MI 48240

Maid of Scandinavia Co.
3244 Raleigh Ave.
Minneapolis, MN 55416

Paprikas Weiss Importer
1546 Second Ave.
New York, NY 10028

H. Roth & Son
Lekvar By The Barrel
1577 First Ave.
New York, NY 10028

Williams-Sonoma
P.O. Box 3792
San Francisco, CA 94119

Index

Almond(s), 7–8
  butter spongecake, 72–73
  orange torte, 83–84
  paste, 171–73
    basic recipe, 172
    decorations, 173
    torte, 96–97
  splinters, 170
  spongecake, 69
  twist, 131–32
Alt Wiener Apfelkuchen, 54–55
Anise cake, 24
Aniskuchen, 24
Apfeldatsche, 125–26
Apfelkuchen
  Alt Wiener, 54–55
  Bayrischer, 58–59
  mit Brosamen, 56–57
  mit Geleeguss, 52–53
  mit Guss, 50–51
  mit Nüssen, 55–56
  mit Quark, 51–52
  mit Schaumguss, 53–54
  Versunkener, 26–27
Apfelmuskuchen, 57–58
Apfelstrudel, 107
Apple(s), 9
  cake, sunken, 26–27
  sheet tart, 125–26
  strudel, 107
  tarts,
    with breadcrumbs, 56–57
    cloud-top, 53–54
    glazed, 52–53
    with nuts, 55–56
    old Vienna, 54–55
    Quark, 51–52
    with souffle filling, 50–51
Applesauce tart, 57–58

Apricot(s)
  preserves glaze, 166
  tart with spongecake topping, 44
  windmills, 118
Aprikosen
  -kuchen mit Biskuithaube, 44
  -radchen, 118

Baking
  equipment, 1–2
    sources of, 176
  sheets, 2
Baumstamm, 71–72
Bavarian apple tart, 58–59
Bayerischer Apfelkuchen, 58–59
Beehive cake, 25–26
  slices, 126
Bienenstich, 25–26
  Schnitten, 126
Birnen
  -kuchen, 50
  -strudel, 107
Biskuit
  basic, 68
  directions for, 63–67
  recipes, 68–74
Biskuitrolle, 70
  mit Schlagsahne, 71
Black Forest cherry torte, 78–79
Blätterteig
  basic, 112
  -boden für Obstkuchen, 114
  directions for, 111–14
  recipes, 114–20
Blueberry(ies)
  brittle tart, 57
  tart, 45–46
  torte, 92–93

Brandteig
  basic, 101
  directions for, 101–102
Butter, 5
  cakes,
    directions for, 11–15
    recipes, 15–28
  spongecakes
    basic, 72
    directions for, 66
    recipes, 72–74
Butterbiskuit
  basic, 72
  directions for, 66
  recipes, 72–74
Buttercreams, 151–52
  basic recipe for, 151
  with custard base, 153
  flavored, 151–52
Buttercreme mit Creme Unterlage, 153

Cake flour, 3
Candied citrus peel, 173–74
Candies, decorative, 167–74
Carrot torte, 86–87
Cheese(s)
  apple tart, 51–52
  cake, one-bowl, 17–18
  cherry tart, 47
  cream torte, 79–80
  pockets, 137–38
  tart, 46–47
Cherry(ies)
  cake, sunken sour, 27–28
  meringue tart, 41
  strudel, 108
  tart, simple, 40
Chocolate, 10
  butter frosting, 165
  butter spongecake, 73
  buttercream with custard base, 153
  cream with whipped cream, 156
  fondant, 163
  frosting with egg white, 165–66
  log, 71–72
  nugget cake, 19
  pralines, 168
  rum cake, 20
  shaved, 173
  spongecake, 69
    roll, 70
  sugar frosting, 164–65
  torte, 82
  truffles, 169

Chocolates, 168–70
Cinnamon snails, 138
Cloud-top apple tart, 53–54
Cocoa, 10
Cookies, 141–47
Cornstarch, 3
  custard, 160–61
Covered puff pastry tart, 115
Cream
  whipping, 5–6
  sour, 6
Cream horns, 117
Cream puffs, 102–103
  pastry
    basic recipe, 101
    directions for, 101–102
Creme(s)
  mit Gelatin, 161
  für Obstkuchen, 160–61
  mit Stärkemehl, 160–61
Crumb
  cake, 18–19
  sheet cake, 126
  topping, 149
Currant(s), 9
  tart, 47–48
Custard filling for tarts, 160–61

Daisy cake, 23
Danish pastry, 136
  recipes, 136–39
Dobos Torte, 95–96
Domed fruit torte, 84–85

Eclairs, 103
Eggs, 3–4
  separating, 3–4
  whites, 4–5
    beating, 4
    folding, 5
Einfache Zuckerglasuren, 164
Einfacher Kirschenkuchen, 40
Erdbeer
  Krokant Kuchen, 57
  Torte, 89

Farina, 3
Filbert(s), 8
  butter spongecake, 72–73
  cake, 17
  meringue cookies, 146
  spongecake, 68
  torte, 81–82
Filled crescents, 138–39

Filled ring cookies, 141–42
Fillings, 149–61
Flache Kuchen
   directions for, 31–38
   recipes, 38–60
Flour, 2–3
Fondant frosting, 161–62
Franchipantörtchen, 61
Frangipane tartlets, 61
Frankfurt Crown, 80–81
Frankfurter Kranz, 80–81
Frostings, 161–66
Frucht-Kuppeltorte, 84–85
Früchtebrot, 132–33
Fruit tartlets, 60–61
Fruitbread, 132–33

Gefüllte Hörnchen, 139
Gefüllter Blätterkuchen, 115
Gekochter Schokoladen-Zuckerguss, 164–65
Gelatin custard, 161
Gelatin *Geleeguss*, 167
Gelatin glaze, 167
Geleegüsse, 166–67
   Gelatin, 167
   Johannisbeer, 167
   Marmeladeglasur, 166
Geraspelte Schokolade, 171
Glasuren, 166–67
Glaze(s)
   apricot preserves, 166
   red currant, 167
   gelatin, 167
Glazed apple tart, 52–53
Glazed rhubarb tart, 59–60
Gooseberry tart, 41–42
Grape tart, 44–45
Gugelhopf, 126–27
   mold, 1
   Rum, 19–20

Haselnuss
   -*biskuit*, 68
   Butter Biskuit, 72–73
   -*kuchen*, 17
   -*makronen*, 146
   -*torte*, 81–82
Hefeboden für Plattenkuchen, 124–25
Hefekranz, 128
Hefeteig
   -*boden für Obstkuchen*, 124
   directions for, 121–23
   recipes, 124–39

Heidelbeer
   -*kuchen*, 45–46
   -*torte*, 92–93
Himbeerbrötchen, 145–46
Hutzelbrot, 132

Icings, 161–66

Jelly roll(s)
   basic recipe, 70
   filling and unmolding, 67
   pan for, 2
   recipes, 70–72
Johannisbeer
   Geleeguss, 167
   -*kuchen*, 47–48

Karottentorte, 86–87
Käsekuchen, 46–47. See also *Quark-Napfkuchen*
Käsesahne-Torte, 79–80
King Cake, 22–23
Kirschenkuchen
   mit Baiserhaube, 41
   Einfacher, 40
   Versunkener, 27–28
Kirschenstrudel, 108
Kleingebäck, 141
   recipes, 141–47
Konfekt, 164–74
Königskuchen, 22–23
Krokant, 170

Lemon(s), 9
   buttercream, 155
   cake, 15
   peel
      candied, 173
      grated, 9
   torte, 97–98
Linzer Torte, 43
Little rascals, 142–43
Loaf pans, 2

Mandel
   -*biskuit*, 69
   Butter Biskuit, 72–73
   -*Orangen-Torte*, 83–84
   -*splitter*, 170
   -*stange*, 131–32
Marble cake, 16–17
Margaretenkuchen, 23
Marillenringe, 141–42
Marmeladeglasur, 166

Marmorkuchen, 16–17
Marzipan, 171
    basic recipe, 172
    decorations, 173
Marzipantorte, 96–97
Mocha torte, 86
Mohnstollen, 134–35
Mokka
    -schnitten, 103
    -torte, 86
Mürbteig
    basic directions and recipes, 31–38
    in tarts and tartlets, 38–61

Napfkuchen, 11
Nougat, 171
    balls, 169
Nougatkugeln, 169
Nuss Butter Biskuit, 72–73
Nusskämme, 118–19
Nut(s), 7–8
    butter spongecake, 72–73
    combs, 118–19
Nutrition, 10

Obstkuchen
    directions for, 31–38
    recipes, 38–60
Obsttörtchen, 60–61
Old Vienna apple tart, 54–55
One-bowl cheese cake, 17–18
Orange(s), 9
    balls, 168–69
    butter spongecake, 74
    buttercream, 155
    cake, 21
    peel
        candied, 173
        grated, 9
    torte, 85–86
    winecream torte, 91–92
Orangeat, 173
Orangen
    Butter Biskuit, 74
    Buttercreme, 155
    -kuchen, 21
    -kugeln, 168–69
    -torte, 85–86
    -Weincreme-Torte, 91–92
Ovens, 2

Palmiers, 120
Pans, 1–2
Pariser Creme, 156–57
Parisian cream, 156–57

Peach(es)
    cream torte, 90–91
    tart, 42
Pear(s)
    strudel, 107
    tart, 50
Pfirsich
    -Cremetorte, 90–91
    -kuchen, 42
Pflaumenkuchen, 48–49
Pistachios, 8
Plum tart, 48–49
Plunderteig
    directions for, 136
    recipes, 136–39
Poppyseed stollen, 134–35
Pound cakes,
    directions for, 11–15
    recipes, 28–30
Prinzregententorte, 94–95
Prune plum(s)
    sheet tart, 125
    strudel, 108
    tart, 49
Puff Pastry
    basic recipe, 112
    directions for, 111–14
    recipes, 114–20
    shell for tarts, 114

Quark
    -Apfelkuchen, 51–52
    apple tart, 51–52
    basic recipe for, 149–51
    cream torte, 79–80
    -Napfkuchen, 17–18
    -stollen, 135–36
    -strudel, 109
    -taschen, 137–38

Raisin(s), 9
    cake with rum, 19–20
Raspberry(ies)
    brittle tart, 57
    cookies, 145–46
Red Currant(s)
    glaze, 167
    tart, 47–48
Rehrücken
    mold for, 1
    torte, 93–94
Rhabarberkuchen, 38–39
    mit Geleegus, 59–60
    mit Haselnüssen, 39–40

Rhabarberstrudel, 108
Rhubarb
   strudel, 108
   tarts, 38–39
      with filberts, 39–40
      glazed, 59–60
Rich tart pastry
   basic directions for, 31–38
   in tarts and tartlets, 32–34
Rolled cake, 128–129
Rührkuchen
   directions for, 11–15
   recipes, 15–30
Rum balls, 168
Rum Gugelhopf, 19–20
Rumkugeln, 168
Rum-raisin cake, 19–20

Sachertorte, 98–99
Saddle of venison mold, 93
Sahnetorte, 82–83
Salt, 7
Sand cake, 28–30
Sandkuchen, 28–30
Schillerlocken, 117
Schlagsahne, 5–6, 157–59
   basic recipe, 158
   flavored, 158–59
   with gelatin, 158
Schmelzender Zuckerguss, 161–62
Schneckennudeln, 138
Schnitzbrot, 132–33
Schokolade Biskuitrolle, 70
Schokoladen
   -*biskuit,* 69
   Butter Biskuit, 73
   -*Buttercreme mit Creme Unterlage,* 153
   -*Butterglasur,* 165
   -*creme mit Schlagsahne,* 156
   -*glasur mit Eiweiss,* 165–66
   -*kuchen,* 19
   mit Rum, 20
   -*torte,* 82
   -*trüffel,* 169
Schwäbischer Kranz, 130–31
Schwarzwälder Kirschtorte, 78–79
Schweinsöhrchen, 120
Serving quantities from tortes, cakes, and spongecake rolls, 77
Shaved chocolate, 171
Simple cherry tart, 40
Simple sugar icings, 164
Slicing tortes and cakes, 77
Spitzbuben, 142–43

Spongecake
   basic, 68
   directions for, 63–67
   recipes, 68–74
   roll with whipped cream, 71
Springform pans, 1
Stachelbeerkuchen, 41–42
Stollen, 133–34
Strawberry(ies)
   brittle tart, 57
   torte, 89
Streusel, 149
Streusel
   -*kuchen,* 18–19
   Schnitten, 126
Strudel, 105–107
   basic, 105
   recipes, 107–109
Sugar(s), 6–7
Sultanas, 9
Sunken apple cake, 26–27
Sunken sour cherry cake, 27–28
Swabian crown, 130–31

Tart(s)
   directions for, 31–38
   recipes, 38–60
   using a fully baked shell, 58–60
Tartlet(s)
   frangipane, 61
   fruit, 60–61
Tausend-Blätter-Torte, 116
Tausendjahrkuchen, 21–22
Tea bread, 144–45
Teebrot, 144–45
Thousand layer torte, 116
Thousand year cake, 21–22
Tiroler Kuchen, 15–16
Toasted almond brittle, 170–71
Tongues, 119–20
Topfkuchen, 11
Toppings, 149–61
Tortes
   general information, 75–77
   recipes, 78–99
Traubenkuchen, 44–45
Trüffel Pralinen, 168
Turk's head mold, 1
Tyrolean cake, 15–16

Vanilla
   cookies, 145
   cream, 154–55
   extract, 8
   sugar, 9

Vanillebrötchen, 145
Versunkener Apfelkuchen, 26–27
Versunkener Sauerkirschenkuchen, 27–28
Viennese chocolate torte, 88–89

Walnuss
   Butter Biskuit, 72–73
   -kuchen, 23–24
Walnut
   butter spongecake, 72–73
   cake, 23–24
Wasp's nests, 146–47
Weisser Zuckerguss, 163
Wespennester, 146–47
Whipped cream, 5–6, 157–59
   basic, 158
   flavored, 158–59
   with gelatin, 158
   torte, 82–83
Wickelkuchen, 128–29

Wiener Schokoladentorte, 88–89
Windbeutel, 102–103

Yeast
   crown, 128
   dough
      base for sheet tarts, 124–125
      directions for, 121–123
      recipes, 124–39
      shell for tarts, 124
   sponge, 122

Zitronat, 173–74
Zitrone Buttercreme, 155
Zitronen
   -kuchen, 15
   -torte, 97–98
Zungen, 119–20
Zwetschgen
   -datsche, 125
   -kuchen, 49
   -strudel, 108